MW01287149

JnJ Publishing House

Real, Practical, and Super-natural; Ministry Resources for the
Next Generation

For Questions or Comments: www.JnJpublishing.com

영어권 사역 목사님

For online orders, questions, or comments:

www.JnJpublishing.com

Hiring an English Ministry Pastor & Beyond

In an Asian American Church context

Joseph Y. Choi
with W. Jae Lee

And contributions from English Ministry Pastors and Asian American Church leaders

www.JnJpublishing.com
email: JnJpublishinghouse@gmail.com

JnJ Publishing House is a Christian publisher dedicated to serving the multicultural and multi-ethnic Christian community in the United States and abroad. We believe God's vision for JnJ Publishing is to provide ministry resources for the next generation of church leaders and Christians, with ministry resources that are "Real, Practical, and Supernatural."

Details in stories have been changed to protect the identities of the persons, church, and ministries involved. Please note that this book is published for information and general circulation purposes only and does not constitute nor purport to constitute any form of advice and recommendation. While the information set out is based on sources believed to be reliable, Joseph Choi, W Jae Lee and JnJ Publishing House makes no representations or warranties expressed or implied as to the accuracy, completeness or timeliness of any such information.

ISBN-13: 978-1467991698
ISBN-10: 1467991694

JnJ Publishing House
Columbia, Maryland, U.S.A.
Printed in the United States of America
2011 – First Edition

Table of Contents

Part 7: Asian American Churches 249

Appendix:

Asian Church Terminology

Korean Ministry KM

- This defines the head church to be 1st immigrant Korean.
- Single Native Language

Chinese Ministry CM

- This defines the head church to be 1st immigrant Chinese.
- Overseas-born Chinese Pastor or OBC Pastor
- American Born Chinese Pastor or ABC Pastor
- Majority in single language

English Ministry EM

-This defines an English speaking ministry that is under the umbrella and control of the 1st immigrant head church.

English Ministry (EM) Pastor

- This defines a minister who is the shepherd over those that are out of high school and primarily speaks English in an Asian American Church context.

First Generation Immigrant (**FiGI**)

- This term is defined as an immigrant that is born outside of North America. The FiGI lifestyle, behavior, language, culture, food, and tradition primarily are from the home land.
- Single Native Language

Asian-American (**AsiAm**)

-By Asian-American we mean primarily the Korean and Chinese churches, because we have little to no experience with other Asian churches.

Head Church

- The word defines the 1st generation immigrant leadership that oversees and governs the English Ministry.

Hiring Church

- Head church that is to be the employer of the potential EM/Youth pastor.

2nd Generation (Gen) Citizens

- A child born from the FiGIs in a new country. The 2nd gen citizen of the new country will contain majority of the lifestyle, behavior, and perspective of the new country while maintaining a small percentage of the culture, food, language, and tradition of the parents' homeland.

1.5 generation of immigrants

- The 1.5 generation (gen) is coined to refer to those who have immigrated to a new country before or during their early teens. The 1.5 gen immigrants bring with them the characteristics of their native country but assimilate and socialize in the new country. Their identity is a combination of the old and new cultures and traditions.
- Somewhat Bilingual

INTRODUCTION

Across from the table sat a 27 year old Korean American woman, who was sobbing about her experience at her previous Korean church. Because of her bad experiences at the 1st generation, Korean American Churches, she decided to attend an American church. However, she felt she was not growing spiritually in the American church where she now attends. She tried hard to participate in the young adult small group, but struggled to give herself fully to the fellowship because of her past experience with two previous Korean church splits. She still maintained a close relationship with her Korean friends whom she grew up with. Hae Young's experience is typical of what many Christian Korean Americans have faced for decades.

Hae Young came to the U.S. at a young age, and like many 1st generation immigrants (FiGIs), her parents eventually bought a small business. They also started attending a church a Korean business associate recommended. There the parents found a community in which the language, food, and culture reminded them of their homeland. The first immigrant church provided not only the gospel message, but a community in which social and political issues from the native homeland were discussed. It was through these first immigrant Korean churches that social events were planned and enjoyed.

This was the environment in which Hae Young grew up. These first immigrant Koreans had children, who grew up learning English. And as these children became college age, the student population within the first immigrant churches began to grow, creating a need to hire an English Ministry (EM) pastor to minister to the growing college and young adult groups. Their youth pastor was already busy running activities and programs for the middle and high school students. However, even with a growing number of youth at this church, youth pastors didn't seem to stay longer than three years. Although some students left the church, many youths decided to stay because their parents stayed.

Hae Young had made many close friends at her past Korean church. But now she attends a university where there are at least one or two Korean-Christian Bible study groups or fellowships where she stays connected to the church. She continues to stay in contact with her parents' church and is even requested to come back on weekends to help with youth and Sunday school ministry. Within a few years of being away at college, she had already witnessed a different EM pastor. A conflict arose between the Korean elders, who ruled the church, and the EM pastor, which eventually led the EM pastor's departure. He was the second EM pastor to have left in the past six years. After her graduation Hae Young decided to stay and live in the area. She is now working full time and assisting her parents' business few days a week and teaching Sunday school at her parents' church.

At the request of her new EM pastor, she started a singles small group for young adult women. A bond was growing between many of the college and young adult members of the EM congregation and within a few years, the EM congregation had grown. Young families were starting to bloom as a growing number of the EM members were getting married. With this increasing number of single professionals, married couples, college students and even non-Koreans, the EM was not unable to fully function on its own under the umbrella of the Korean Church. With only one building many of the events that the EM wanted to host would interfere with the Korean ministries and cause a scheduling war between the two. As a result the conflict between the two ministries became more like a turf war, and Hae Young was asked to come into an important meeting.

The meeting took place with many of the EM core members. Frustrations surfaced concerning the leadership style and the authoritativeness of the KM in dictating the programs of the church. Even having joint services three or four times a year with the KM and EM were starting to become a burden for the EM's vision and mission. Since these joint services were conducted in Korean, many non-Korean speaking members of the EM did not feel comfortable attending, and the second gen Korean Americans had difficulty inviting their non-Asian friends because they felt that their non-Korean speaking friends would feel disconnected. There were cultural concerns as well, such as the smell of the precious Korean side dish "kim-chee." A monthly meeting took place with the EM core team members and then another conflict arose between the new senior KM pastor and the EM pastor that escalated the situation.

The new KM pastor wanted more control of the entire church, including the EM, where as the previous senior KM pastor had more of a hands off approach because of his experience with past EM pastors. This was a clear sign for the EM to depart and become an independent church plant. A request was made from the EM pastor to depart and plant an independent church. The elders and the new KM pastor denied the proposition. One of the primary fears of KM was that if the EM congregation left, they would be taking the majority of the Sunday school and youth teachers with them.

Nevertheless, the EM pastor submitted his resignation to the new KM pastor and set the date with the core team along with many others, including the majority of the married couples and professionals, to plant a new independent EM church. Hae Young was fed up with the politics of the KM and decided to follow the EM pastor and the exciting new direction of her Christian life.

The independent EM church did not go well in its first year, and when the Pastor was offered another EM position at a different state, he left the infant church to struggle on its own. The congregation rallied to stay together, but with few people leaving here and there, the core team decided it no longer had the funds to hire another pastor nor stay afloat with the current trend in the church tithing. The difficult decision was made to dissolve the church.

I sat there shaking my head. I knew exactly what she was talking about. Though my experience was from another state at another time, everything she said resonated with my heart. I knew her frustration and her emotional pain. From being a Sunday school teacher myself to eventually becoming an EM pastor, I clearly understood the internal church struggles and conflicts of the Korean American Church, and many if not all AsiAm churches have similar issues.

Undoubtedly, the dialog for a resolution has been going on in various parts of the country as more and more church leaders run into these issues. Whether they have resolved those issues or abdicated to their difficulties remains in their own situations. The rest of us didn't have the benefit of learning from their experience. The purpose for writing this book was to open up the discussion on a broader scale and begin formulating a solution to the ministry struggles that KMs and EMs face. By increasing awareness and opening the communication lines, we want to bridge the gap that separates the 1st generation immigrant (FiGI) head churches and the EM pastors so that long-term unity between the two may be the norm instead of the exception. Cultural and philosophical differences don't have to preclude effective ministry in the FiGI church, whether the EM is independent or not. Thank you for entering into the discussion by purchasing this book.

Primary Objective

For years we have seen our struggling brothers and sisters in Christ lose their faith in the Korean American church. Some migrate to an American church while others take a break from attending. Others have rejected church entirely, and some have even jettisoned their faith in Jesus all because they saw the politics of the leadership encumbering the ministry, leaving a wake of disillusioned sheep. Can we set a better example? We must. In obedience to Christ, we must be unified. There is no other alternative.

As 1.5 gen Korean American pastors, we have a desire to unite the body of believers, especially the first and second gen Asian Americans (AsiAm) churches. We envision greater camaraderie with bicultural, multi-generational, FiGI and EM pastors as they discuss the matters we bring up. Not that these issues haven't been introduced before, but we are encouraging the open dialog that need to take place if we are to intentionally move forward in the pursuit of unity and greater ministry effectiveness. Conflicts debilitate the ministry and cause collateral damage. What a shame it is when the very ones who were assigned to bring the flock together cause them to flee. As leaders we must do better. Let us pull together.

All the research, surveys, observations, interviews, and personal experiences in this book were included to dissect the issues that cause conflict in the AsiAm church. Before the EM candidate is hired and before the EM position is accepted, the matters addressed in this book should be considered. The questions at the end of the "Part" segments will guide both parties as they consider working together.

We realize this book is more than twenty years too late, but for those of us still struggling with these issues, it's right on time. Besides, history has a way of vengefully repeating itself so it may yet be useful as a ministry resource. Consider the generous feedback below:

Part of my ministry is to assist and facilitate the planting of new Asian American churches. Choi and Lee's book "Hiring an EM pastor" breaks new ground in this new frontier of American church planting. There is no other book written which is as comprehensive and practical on the subject of the nuts and bolts of planting and staffing an Asian American English speaking church. For anyone who wants to know more about this subject I recommend that you read and put its principles into practice. - Dr. Ron Blankenship, Director of Missions/Church Planting Catalyst for Montgomery Baptist Association in MD and Adjunct Professor of Missions at Washington Baptist University.

"God, give us grace to accept with serenity
the things that cannot be changed,
Courage to change the things
which should be changed,
and the Wisdom to distinguish
the one from the other.
"Living one day at a time,
Enjoying one moment at a time,
Accepting hardship as a pathway to peace,
Taking, as Jesus did,
This sinful world as it is,
Not as I would have it,
Trusting that You will make all things right,
If I surrender to Your will,
So that I may be reasonably happy in this life,
And supremely happy with You forever in the next."
-   Reinhold Niebuhr

Part 1

The

Beginning

1

The Beginning

Hae Young's story is an experience common in many Asian American churches. The devastating splits and disillusionment that follows frequently result in an intense dislike for the 1st generation (gen) immigrant church for many Asian Americans (AsiAm) who grew up under this environment. Like so many others Hae Young longed for a church that would model unity and minister to her spiritual needs. Whenever Hae Young recollects her experience, she shows physical manifestations of her emotional pain. She looks quite disturbed and goes through stomach pangs. Although this may be extreme, it highlights the need to prevent the causes that triggered it. Many in her situation never go back to a Korean church and some even leave the church altogether because of the "politics" that occur there.

Recently, a friend of mine moved because of his job. John came to the U.S. at an early age and experienced first-hand the issues of the Korean American church, but after he got married and had three children, he wanted to get reconnected to the Korean community and especially to a Korean church.

John and his wife found a good EM church located near there temporary home. He found the church on the web, and it appeared to be a solid EM community. When the Lees attended their very first service, the EM pastor announced that he was leaving in a few weeks. This devastated the Lee family. They just came out of a situation in California where their Korean church was in disarray because the KM and EM pastors had issues, and now they were faced with a similar problem on the opposite side of the country.

Apparently, when the EM pastor was first hired, there was an agreement between the senior KM pastor and the EM pastor to eventually bless the EM congregation to become fully independent as a new church plant. However, when the previous KM pastor was ousted out by the elders, the new KM pastor wanted the EM to be under the control of the Head Church. This did not fare well with the EM pastor who moved out with 25-30% of the EM congregation.

So what are the roots of the problem? How can we solve these conflicts that continue to arise in many AsiAm churches across the United States? Is there anything that we can do to minimize these causes of conflicts? What are some practical solutions to these issues? This section will look deep into the hiring practices of AsiAm churches in order to understand the mindset of the 1st gen church leaders.

When my wife and I ran into a good friend from college, he invited us to attend his EM church. He let me know that they had just started this English Ministry with the KM pastor leading the sermons in English. I thought this was very unusual because most KM pastors do not speak English well, let alone give a sermon in English. My friend started attending this church because the children's department desperately needed some help from English speaking 1.5 and 2nd gen Korean Americans to teach the children. Prompted by their 1st generation (gen) parents and desiring to serve in some way, the English speaking young adults and couples became Sunday school teachers and small group leaders. However, they weren't very motivated to attend the worship service where only Korean was spoken. When the senior pastor noticed this, he wanted to provide something that would be more relevant to them. Thus their EM was born.

Thankfully, this new 1.5 gen KM pastor was a former U.S. soldier and spoke English well. I was surprised at first about his English speaking skills and his ability to relate to the newly formed EM congregation. Though we were small in number, the congregation grew, albeit slowly. The KM and EM eventually grew to the point where the pastor's time was needed more in the larger Korean Ministry.

With the KM pastor's encouragement, the EM began searching for an EM pastor to take the growing EM congregation to the next level. This particular EM congregation was made up of mostly young married couples and single professionals with a few college students. However, in many Korean churches that are seeking their first EM pastor, there are only a few married couples and professionals. College students are the majority.

Many in our core EM had Master's degrees with some professional experience. Some were small business owners who contributed to our decision-making process in hiring an EM pastor. Through prayer, analyzing resumes, and interviews we were able to find a solid 1.5 gen EM pastor, who was married with children, to lead our growing EM congregation. This EM pastor led over ten years and grew the EM. However, finding the right EM pastor for many AsiAm churches is a struggle and for some with a high turn-over rate among EM/Youth pastors', giving up is easier to do than to fill the need of the church.

The Need

There is a shortage of EM pastors in Korean and Chinese churches throughout the United States as well other countries like Canada and Australia. EM pastors are also in high demand in South Korea where large churches now hold English worship services for many foreigners who English speaking and those desiring to learn English.

The Los Angeles Times article reads, *"Asian American churches are going through a 'crisis of leadership' because seminaries are not preparing a new generation of pastors to work in multi-generational and multi-cultural settings, Asian American Christian leaders say."*[1]

Comprehensive statistics on the shortage of EM pastors are very difficult to come by, but many indicators do show that there are not enough EM pastors for the churches that need them. Due to the lack of 1.5 and 2nd gen EM pastors, other ethnic pastors are filling the roles. I have a friend who was born and raised in Jamaica now serving as the EM pastor of a Chinese church. A Jamaican serving in a Chinese church was big news in the past, but with the demand growing each month, churches are willing to hire non-Asians to lead their EM. At a large Korean American youth rally, the primary speaker was a Caucasian, who was an EM pastor at a Korean church. With such a small number of EM pastors available many smaller Korean American churches now have college lay leaders stepping up to serve the children and teens. But they usually burn out because the work is overwhelming and they are often undertrained. Smaller AsiAm churches are not able to hire a full-time EM pastor, so either a lay leader with at least some English speaking ability acts as the shepherd and Bible study leader or a part-time EM or Youth pastor is hired.

Immigrant churches normally go through the traditional method of networking with people in order to find an EM pastor or a lay leader to help with the English Ministry. Even to this day, this is still a common practice. While non-Asians who graduated from seminary are having some difficulty in finding positions, many Asians studying to be pastors are approached even during seminary with ministry offers. While I was attending seminary, two Korean churches approached me to offer positions. Other 1.5 and 2nd gen ministers are sought out if they are not serving at any Asian church.

In the early stages of the immigrant church history, any lay leader who was able to speak English was qualified to teach any English-speaking group. Now, with the growth of the number of 1.5, 2nd, and 3rd gen AsiAm pastors, churches have to be more intentional about hiring qualified and experienced ministers. But the demand for pastors does not just come from growing AsiAm churches. They come from the vacancies left by previous pastors who have gone to serve somewhere else. The vacancies are caused by many 1st gen Head Churches and its lay leaders who are not prepared to handle conflicts when they arise. Neither are the majority of the EM pastors.

Explained further in the leadership section of this book is the reality that the majority of the 1st gen KM pastors and Head Church leaders come from a strict, structured, and competitive society. South Korean men enter a mandatory military service, where mental and physical discipline is reinforced through a structured environment. There, conflict and strife are discouraged, and unity and order are cultivated. The men bring that lifestyle back to their families and jobs.

This is the reason why in a homogeneous society like Asia, foreigners, those who were racially mixed, and even 2nd gen non-natives who have not been exposed to the lifestyle face difficulty interacting and responding to a uniform culture. That homogeneous mentality, nature, and culture is brought to America and battles with a society that is less disciplined and more individualistic. Therein lie the reasons many conflicts arise between the 2nd gen and 1st gen AsiAm pastors. Two very different almost opposite cultures are trying to coexist on equal terms.

Can dual ministries with differing philosophies exist in harmony and become effective and successful under one roof? A resounding "Yes" is our reply, with a caveat. We suggest practical ways in which two differing cultures can grow into a unified church.

Understanding the Primary Issues before Hiring

Before hiring an EM pastor understanding the primary causes of conflicts between members of different generations can greatly reduce the chance of serious conflicts and bring greater unity in the church leadership. Even with numerous offers, many young AsiAm pastors are discouraged by the possibility of working with First Generation Immigrant (FiGI) churches. The LA Times article noted, *"Pastors, seminary professors and lay leaders said at the session and in later interviews that generational schisms in Asian American churches are causing clergy attrition and turnover among pastors born or reared in the United States."* The article continues, *"Some young pastors experience so much frustration that they start their own English-speaking, pan-Asian churches. Others become so disillusioned that they leave the ministry, experts said."*[2]

The LA Times continues to cite a 2005 Duke Divinity School study called, "Asian American Religious Leadership Today," which indicates that the primary reason for tensions arise out of *"cultural differences"* in the styles and philosophies of church leadership. The FiGI hierarchal structure is difficult to handle for many EM pastors.

Even without comprehensive data on why AsiAm churches face conflict, there is so much consensus among leaders and members of AsiAm churches that we will delineate major areas that we have noticed coming up in conversations and complaints. The five primary reasons why an EM pastor gets discouraged enough to leave the FiGI church are:

1. Conflicts between FiGI head church pastor and head church leaders. (Miscommunication, lack of communication, unexpressed expectations, and lack of transparency)

2. Cultural and generational differences producing different ministry philosophies. A bi-cultural ministry under one church. We named this GCM-D (Generational & Cultural Ministry philosophy Differences).

3. EM lacking power, voice, and control

4. Different visions

5. Lack of cooperation and community effort from the Head Church leadership and body.

In private many expressed a concern over the amount of financial support they were receiving from many of the Head Churches. This would be an area not mentioned in the above list which may cause an EM pastor's departure from a KM. Many do not want to just minister for the sake of a "paycheck," so dialogue in this area is minimal even among the EM pastors. However, it is still important in the overall decision making process of hiring an EM pastor because although it is not the primary issue for EM pastors looking for another ministry, it does become an important unexpressed matter, especially for those with family.

Many 1st gen Head Churches believe strongly that no one should be getting paid more than the senior pastor. So eventually, when the finances do become an issue for the EM pastor's family where either the pastor or his wife has to look for a part-time or full-time job to cover family expenses, the pastor will leave if another church offers a higher pay. Financial concerns play a major role in cases because the EM pastor has to provide for the needs of his family. Pastors will always trust and rely on God to provide for all areas of their lives, but the churches must provide a suitable environment in which the basic needs such as finances are met so it doesn't interfere with the pastor's ministry efforts or focus. Part 4 "Pastor's Salary" will give an expanded perspective on this subject.

In light of the major causes of conflict between the first and second gen pastoral leadership, we would like to suggest and recommend several things in order to improve the relationship between generations. But even before the prescription of how to avoid or work through conflicts, we would like to shed some light on the subject of interpersonal dynamics, and cultural thought patterns between the generations.

Chapter 1

The Search

We are seeking a Pastor that will . . .

In evaluating over 50 different ads for hiring an EM pastor position, there are some common denominators in the words being used. The following are samples and combined descriptions of what was advertised by Korean and Chinese Churches from the state of California to New Jersey and everywhere in between.

The following major sources were the used along with others:

1. Korean-American Ministry Resources
2. MinistryList.com
3. ChurchStaffing.com

Note: Church names and locations were not used to assess the data, just the job descriptions and the congregation size. A few of the source information was combined due to the length of the script or lack thereof. A number of ads did not specify the age and size of the congregation. In these cases the information was obtained through the church's website in order to determine the general category of the congregation.

Sample Descriptions:
Position/Job

Illinois: The position would involve <u>preaching</u> during the weekly Sunday Worship service, <u>pastoral care</u> of members, <u>supervision</u> of lay staff, <u>management</u> of fellowship events and ministries, and <u>discipling</u> of individual members of congregation.

Congregation: We have a native language congregation of about 160 attendees and an English-speaking congregation of about 100 attendees. The English congregation consists of 80% young families, about 20% young career, and 10% youth.

California: The pastor will <u>lead</u>, <u>minister</u> to and <u>nurture</u> the <u>spiritual growth</u> of the English Ministry.

Congregation: The English ministry of 30 members represents various cultures, age groups and ethnicities bound by a common language and the vision of the parent church.

New Jersey: We are seeking a pastor to <u>lead</u> and <u>shape</u> the youth and college group.

Congregation: Congregation contains mainly youth and college students.

Canada: Pastor who holds to the authority of the Word of God, the leading of the Holy Spirit, and who is called to exercise <u>spiritual leadership.</u>

Congregation: English speaking second generation.

California: EM pastor with a clear calling and conviction to serve God by <u>leading</u> and <u>supporting</u> the <u>spiritual growth</u> of the congregation.

Congregation: Church does not have an established English Ministry. It will be like building a new church from the ground up by mobilizing the existing English-speaking adults and establishing a foundation for EM.

California: We are praying for a shepherd who has a desire and clear calling to serve God by <u>leading</u> and <u>supporting</u> the <u>spiritual growth</u> of our EM congregation.

Congregation: Our EM congregation currently consists of mainly 1.5 and 2nd generations. We are made up of approximately 150 members, ranging in age from college students to married couples with young children.

North Carolina: Seeking a pastor to <u>lead</u>, <u>manage</u>, <u>supervise</u>, and <u>minister</u> to EM congregation. We desire a pastor that will personally pursue a maturing relationship with Christ and set a Christ-like example in words and actions. The pastor must be able to <u>motivate</u>, <u>encourage</u>, <u>counsel</u> and <u>plan</u> and <u>coordinate</u> events, missions and participate in other general duties.

Congregation: Mostly youth to college and young adults.

Virginia: We seek a pastor who will <u>lead</u>, <u>shape</u>, <u>inspire</u> and <u>encourage</u> our congregation.

Congregation: Our congregation currently consists of a predominantly 1.5 and 2nd gen Korean-American group of about 60-70 members, ranging in age from college students to married couples with young children.

New York: The EM Director is to provide <u>spiritual care</u> and <u>ministry leadership</u> through direct oversight and/or delegation, with the overall responsibility. The EM Director <u>oversees</u> and <u>leads</u> the English worship service on Sundays, and various small group Bible studies and <u>leadership training</u> of each group. The EM Director is subject to the guidance and direction of the Senior Pastor, and works in partnership with the Session.

Congregation: Our congregation currently has 20-25 young adults and graduate students with 70-90 College students.

Texas: The EM pastor will <u>lead</u>, <u>direct</u> and be <u>responsible</u> for our EM services and activities, as well as be the <u>spiritual educator</u> and <u>leader</u> of our youth, including the youngest of youths, to our senior adults, who are English-speaking.

Congregation: The EM pastor will need to establish a new English Ministry, it will be like building a new church from the ground up by mobilizing the existing English-speaking adults and establishing a foundation for EM.

Washington: Our church is seeking a full-time EM pastor to <u>help</u> <u>establish</u> an English Ministry by <u>shepherding</u> and <u>ministering</u> to our college students and youth group.

Congregation: Youth group to college.

Oregon: We are seeking a full-time pastor to <u>lead</u> and <u>grow</u> the English Ministry.

Congregation: The EM consists of 20 young adults, 40 Jr. High and High school students, 70 elementary school age, and 40 pre-K and younger.

Commonly Used Words for Hiring

The following are the words used by the 1st gen Head Church or the Hiring Church in describing what they wanted in the EM pastor candidate. The review of the desires or job descriptions begins with the most stated down to the least stated.

1. Lead
2. Spiritual growth
3. Grow
4. Minister / shepherd
5. Train / develop / shape
6. Shepherd
7. Nurture / counsel
8. Oversee
9. Direct
10. Establish

In analyzing the data it is clear that the majority of the Head Church primarily desires the EM pastor to "lead", guide in "spiritual growth", and "grow" the EM congregation. Based upon the data, the smaller size churches desires the EM pastor to focus more on leading, growing, training, and developing lay leaders, and planning of programs and events. The larger churches want the pastor to lead and grow the congregation toward spiritual maturity with nurture and counsel while overseeing other ministries.

This is a clear indication that when a church grows in its season of life, different leaders play different roles in assisting the church to reach the next level. The church should recognize its season of life to determine whether it should be looking for a visionary to lead the church or a shepherd to grow the spiritual level of the congregation. *However, it should be noted that the Head Church should not expect the newly hired pastor to do both.* Very few leaders have both skill sets, and yet many hiring churches place this expectation on the pastor to fulfill these areas of the job description. The conflict is built in before the pastor has been hired.

George Barna, president of a premiere Christian research firm, notes, *"Another key insight from our research is that most pastors neither see themselves as leaders nor aspire to be leaders. In a recent national survey of protestant senior pastors, we asked them to identify their spiritual gifts. Only 12 % said they have the gift of leadership. In contrast two-thirds of pastors surveyed said they have the gift of teaching or preaching. They have accurately recognized that teaching and leading are two very distinct responsibilities and activities that require different skills that produce differing results."*[3]

> The church should recognize its season of life to determine if the Head Church is looking for a visionary to lead the church or a shepherd to grow the spiritual level of the congregation.

So how do you determine the season of life that a church is in? How do you identify the characteristics of the church? What is the identity of the church? In many cases the identity of the church can attract those who desire to be part of the core value, even when the church is in its infant stages of growth and cannot afford to pay a pastor. By looking deep inside the church and its people, we can find the identity of the church.

Chapter 2

Show Me Your ID

The identity of our church is . . .

A few times when I was driving a bit over the speed limit, a police officer pulled me over. The majority of those times, I felt I was not going over the speed limit but just following the other vehicles in front of me. Nevertheless, each time I was pulled over, the officer asked me to give him my driver's license and the registration for my car. The driver's license indicated who I was and the car registration was used to determine if the car belonged to me. Without a driver's license a person can be severely penalized because the officer will not be able to identify who the person is. Every person, organization, and ministry has a driver's license indicating who or what they are. Names might be different but each person and organization has an identity.

Identity

The abbreviation ID stands for "identification." Every ministry has a unique "ID" or core values associated with their ministries that identifies them. When people think of Billy Graham, they automatically think of "evangelism." Christians bring their non-believing family members and friends to Billy Graham's revivals knowing precisely that evangelism will take place. In essence many Christians associate Billy Graham's identity with evangelism. Benny Hinn's ministry is healing, and for The Brooklyn Tabernacle church it is prayer and a powerful and inspirational worship team. Many will identity Willow Creek Community as a seeker friendly church with strong Leadership Summit conferences, while Saddleback Valley Church is "Purpose Driven." Mosaic Church of Central Arkansas and Bridgeway Community Church in Columbia, Maryland is well known and identified as the forerunner in multi-ethnic and multicultural ministries.

The famous Brooklyn Tabernacle Church, home of the famed Brooklyn Tabernacle Choir is known throughout the world for the several hundred member choir, but for many Christian leaders, the Brooklyn Tabernacle Church is an example of how to grow a church through the power of prayer.

I interviewed an American pastor, whose church was in its fourth year, while he was passing the difficult three year mark during which time many church plants fail. Before planting his church, he spent a few years intensely researching church planting and defining the core values of his future church, all the while praying like his life depended on it. Now his church is reaching its seventh year and going strong. What is central to this church is its identity of "missions."

The overarching goal of a church plant is primarily to establish its vision and mission. People who can identify with its overarching goal will eventually become the make-up of the church. Bridgeway Community Church in Columbia, Maryland has many great ministry programs; however, the priority of being multicultural is placed as its overarching goal. When a certain ministry has a predominant race, their leadership team is encouraged to recruit people of other races and cultures. An intentional recruitment of people of other races stems from its overarching goal.

A 1.5 gen Korean American pastor in Texas designated 40% of their tithing directly to missions. When asked why they were setting aside so much to missions, his response was that it was the church's vision and goal from its inception to make sure that they would play a part in God's Great Commission. After further dialog with this pastor, I realized that it was in the pastor's heart to take part in the Great Commission, and he wanted to show it tangibly. What identifies this ministry is "missions support."

A church in Korea has over 15,000 members and for decades has not purchased their own building but focused on their primary or overarching goal. The identity of this church is to support other ministers and pastors in planting churches either in Korea or other countries. Pastoral interns are trained in this church to primarily go out and either plant churches or focus on missions. Both goals are given strong financial support. This Korean church's identity and core value is church planting.

The subject of identity is an issue for many churches that started as an EM under the umbrella of the Head Church but then became a fully independent church plant. It used to have an identity linked with the Head Church called the "English Ministry," but when they transitioned into a fully independent church plant, the congregation members within the church faced an identity crisis. Questions like these arose: "Who are we now? Are we still a 2nd gen EM church? Do we try to become a multi-ethnic church? Whom are we going to serve as a church?" These and other questions surface causing the church to scramble for a new identity as a fully independent church.

Here is a short excerpt from a church that became an "independent church plant" from a 1st gen Head Church lay leader. [Full story on Part 7 Asian Church Models]

> *What started off with high hopes in the beginning became somewhat diminished over the years when reality set upon a young and inexperienced church. The reality is that just because you want to become a multi-ethnic church doesn't mean that is what you are. The fact is, our Asian church was a niche church that catered to 1.5 and 2nd generation Koreans. Although there were many non-Koreans that came through the doors, most or all did not stay long. Not that we didn't try. As a matter of fact, sometimes we tried too hard. Focusing all our energy to make sure they felt right at home; however, over time they left for various reasons.*
>
> *- Lay Leader*

It is crucial to have an identity that a church can calls its own. The identity fosters unity, and the vision and mission keep it focused on its task. Like the uniforms of any team sport, a church's identity lets the members know whose team they are on and that each must participate fully in order to win. In the case of the church it is to accomplish its mission, which is to impact and influence the community and the world with the gospel.

Recommended Steps:

1. Survey the hiring committee to see what everyone considers to be the church identity.
2. Survey the core team, which will be spending the majority of the time with the new pastor.
3. Survey the entire congregation that the pastor will be preaching to and leading.
4. Have at least two to three primary facilitators to conduct this research. It is important to survey the leadership first and then the congregation. Do not reveal the result until everyone has completed and turned in the survey. In some cases, the identity description from the leadership will be different than that of the congregation, thus the reason for separate survey.

_____

_____

_____

A recommendation about the survey:

It is best to describe the identity of the church in as few words as possible. A driver's license will contain few words and some numbers such as height, weight, age, expiration date, and license number along with the person's name and address. Not much is needed to precisely identify the driver, so minimal words are highly encouraged.

Understanding Core Values

Core values are the central beliefs we hold dear and are foundational reasons why we do what we do. As individuals we have them, as families we have them, as governments we have them, and as churches we also have them. Core values are the preferences or choices churches make in their life together and establish the behavior of the values as the culture of the church. The way a church behaves reflects what the culture of the church is and what the congregation truly values. Core values are not an idea, a program or a goal. Core values are reflected in the consistent choices we make in our church on a daily, monthly, and yearly basis.

A Korean American church in the East coast highly regards prayer as their essential and vital core value. Inside their new church building, a large prayer center was built for over 150 people to gather in corporate prayer. Along the sides were over 20 individual rooms for individual and partner prayers. A prayer director works in conjunction with intercessors and congregation members to pray for their people, community, state, nation and for the gospel message to spread all over the world through their prayers. Early morning prayers for all their leadership team, evening prayers, outreach prayers and countless other ministry programs are all under the covering of daily, weekly, and monthly prayers. For this church their culture and core value is prayer

Core values are not operating practices or strategies. These support the core values. Core values determine how something is done. The priority that is placed on an area of ministry is guided by the core values. Churches with ambiguous core values can result in:

- Church planning has no strong focus or direction which can lead to poor planning
- Confusion among the staff and lay leadership teams
- Decision-making is timid and very slow
- Preoccupation with trivial matters
- Constant squabbling over matters of personal taste
- Decisions constantly deferred
- Traditions keep churches from moving forward
- Wrong "culture" of the church can be created

For this reason the core values must be delineated and discussed with the body. Everyone must be in agreement with the core values in order to be in harmony with one another. So, what are your core values?

Core values are the central beliefs we hold dear and are the foundational reasons why we do what we do.

Here are some questions to ask your EM congregation in order to determine what they say are your core values:

1. What governs our relationships with one another?

2. What values guide our church / ministry process?

3. What values reflect who we are?

4. What values articulate what we stand for?

5. What values explain "why we do ministry the way we do it?"

6. What values guide or direct us in the way we teach and inform people?

7. What values assist and guide us in making the right decisions based upon our vision?

8. What values underpin our church's organization?

9. What values are crucial to our church and ministries?

Recommendation:

If you are a part of the hiring committee as a minister, pastor, ministry professional, or lay leader, I strongly recommend you doing the following assignment first and then doing it as a group. Record each core value on a flash card or white board, and then have each member "rank" the values with 1, 2, or 3 in terms of the priority needed by the ministry with 1 indicating the most important value and 3 being the least important. Then go through the cards again to rank how people think the values are actually being practiced in the church or ministry with 1 indicating the value being fully practiced and 3 indicating hardly at all. It is important to note that core values are not ideals but actual behaviors that create the culture of the church.

This simple process can begin by answering some basic questions. Describe "Who you are" by answering the following questions:

1. Individually I believe (this) or (these) to be my foundational beliefs.

   _____

   _____

   _____

   _____

2. Organizationally we believe (this) or (these) to be our foundational or core value(s).

   _____

   _____

   _____

   _____

3. Are we visually seeing the core values being applied in our ministry / church?

   _____

   _____

   _____

   _____

Overarching Goal

Every church has goals that it desires to fulfill either during the tenure of the pastor or in the lifetime of the church. However, when a church places an "Overarching Goal" as the primary focus, the smaller goals takes a back seat. A church might want to focus on community service and other outreach programs, but without a primary objective it just becomes a program without any real effectiveness.

Many years ago, I served in an outreach ministry targeting homeless adults along with thirty other Christian churches. The center focused on serving by providing hot meals, showers, laundry, a food pantry, clothing, and fellowship. As months passed I noticed that no one brought anyone to Christ nor saw anyone praying with the homeless people. Everyone serving at the homeless center was a dedicated believer in Jesus Christ, yet in a matter of months the visible signs of Christ's presence diminished to almost nothing. I asked myself, "What is the difference between this Christian ministry and a secular humanitarian aid organization? Nothing!"

I decided to step up and pray with people and when the opportunity was opened by the Holy Spirit, I evangelized. Later, I received a phone call from the director asking me not to evangelize because he feared we could be "offending someone who does not believe in what we believe." I found out that evangelism was not the primary goal of the center. In fact, connecting the homeless to Christ was not written anywhere in their overarching goal.

Serving the poor with great food and dignified clothing does not help them get to heaven. The mission and the goals of the center had a tremendous impact in serving the poor but without an "overarching goal" to share the gospel or bring one to Christ so that a permanent home can be reserved upon his death, no real transformation will take place. If all the volunteers understood the overarching goal of "serving with prayer" or "serving bread and sharing Christ" then the center, along with serving food and clothes, would know why they were ministering to the homeless. Their purpose in serving would be clear. Eventually, some homeless people passed away never having received the gospel message because when the opportunity to share the love of Jesus was there, the believers were not permitted.

In seminary, a friend of mine had a passion for music but he always felt regret for not honoring God more with his gift. He was the worship leader at his church and helped many others develop their musical gift for the Lord, but he still felt something was missing. He also had a heart to reach people with the gospel as a minister, but he didn't have the confidence to try. Although he set a goal for the year to honor God with his music, he didn't know how to accomplish it. I applied my researching skills and found a local community college where 5% of the student body were foreigners, who came here to learn English. We started a "music missions" or "M & M" ministry program where we taught students how to sing American songs. At each session we chose three songs, the first two being secular music and the third being a Christian song. With each song, the class went over verbal soundings to match the English words and by the time we came to our third song, we asked simple questions relating to Christian terms. This helped us begin a dialogue about our faith in Jesus Christ. My friend was able to use his ability in music, but having an overarching goal of "reaching the lost within our community with music" gave his gift greater meaning.

When looking for a new pastor, churches begin with their needs. This is reasonable and intuitive, but if the church has an overarching goal of "missions" and "community outreach" but hires a pastor that has a personal overarching goal of "teaching" with smaller goals of community outreach and missions, then conflicts will eventually arise. If the church has an overarching goal of "reaching the lost" or evangelism, then it would be ideal to find a pastor with similar goals and passions.

Core values, vision, mission, and strategies will sometimes change creating a different church identity. This is good if the leaders desire a new direction, but if the members are steadfast in their original overarching goal for the church because their core values haven't changed, the leadership must first sway the congregation before bringing in a pastor who doesn't share the congregation's core values.

An intentional multiracial church was looking to hire a youth pastor. Their goal was to hire someone who was non-white to give the church leadership the multicultural mix. But before looking at the pictures of the potential candidates, they first looked at the ministers' primary goals in life as followers of Jesus Christ and the answer to the question: "If you were given only one work of service for Christ, what would that be and why?"

If the answers matched the core values and the overarching goal of the church, then pictures of the candidates were examined. Similar values and goals between the pastor and the Hiring Church is a recipe for longevity and vitality of their relationship.

The following questions can help you and your church understand and establish overarching goals.

1. The crucial ministry goals our church has helps us become more _____.

2. The overarching goal of _____ gives us purpose and vision that is easily recognized by the regular congregation members.

3. Church members and regular attendees perceive becoming a _____ as being an essential element needed to achieve other goals such as community service, missions, outreach, and etc.

Core Values + Overarching Goal = Identity

Chapter 3

The Passion that Drives

What motivates you?

I attended a leadership conference with many prominent and popular Christian speakers. Thousands of people from all over the world were inspired by the great line of speakers. Every one of them had something important and intriguing to say. Each speaker was very captivating and spoke with zeal. The most fascinating aspect of each speaker was that each and every one of them was very excited about the things they did or the ministry work they were in. After the conference, I went home and wrote in my journal concerning the speakers. The questions I asked myself were, "How did they become who they are today? What drove them to succeed even in the midst of difficulty and trials in their lives? What is the one universal thought or behavior that drives them?" During prayer the frequent thought of the word "passionate" kept coming up. I soon realized the common denominator with all the speakers was that each one had "passion." This was the driving force behind everyone's success in business, career, or ministry. "PASSION" was the singular word that described the success of each speaker.

The identity of Compassion International began with a passion to serve the poor in South Korea. Compassion was founded in 1952 and is one of the world's largest Christian child development agencies, partnering with more than 65 denominations and thousands of local churches to serve more than 800,000 children in 24 countries.

> If there was only one word that would describe the success of every leader who was at the leadership conference, it would be "PASSION."

Evangelist Everett Swanson was invited to speak to the troops in the Republic of Korean army and during the visit he encountered little children sleeping under rags. During the night, military soldiers would search the land and shake the rags to see if any children had died; the soldiers placed the dead children in the back of the truck and departed. There in the midst of the poverty-stricken, war-torn country, something was brewing in the heart of the evangelist. Upon his return to America two checks were handed to Reverend Swanson to help the orphaned children of Korea, evidence to the evangelist that it was God's calling for his life.

After Swanson came another man with the passion to help poverty-stricken children. His name is Dr. Wess Stafford. He became the new president and CEO of Compassion International. He is an internationally recognized advocate for children in poverty. As a child growing up as a missionary's son he personally witnessed his African friends dying from the ravages of war and poverty. He was even abused along with his classmates at a school for missionary children. He then pledged in his heart to fight the mistreatment of children.

His childhood sparked a passion for serving the poor and to speak on behalf of those who could not speak for themselves. In 1977, Wess Stafford joined Compassion International and his passion to help the children in poverty was very prominent at the leadership conference that I attended.

"Compassion and I are a perfect match," Wess says. *"Their philosophy of development reflects everything my experience told me was true — the importance of preserving the dignity of the poor, focusing on empowering people by equipping them rather than doing for them and enhancing cultures by enabling the local church to disciple children. If Compassion had not already existed, I would have had to create it!"*[4] The identity of Compassion International matched perfectly with the passion of Wess Stafford.

Wess Stafford (Passion) + Compassion International (Identity) =
Right Match / Right Fit

> The passion of the leader plus the Identity of the organization results in the right match for God's determined destiny.

What is your passion in life?

What motivates you?

What brings consistent joy and happiness?

What was Apostle Paul's passion in life?

Do you relate to any of the Bible figures and their passion?

Passion-Filled Life

To truly understand a "passion" for Christ, one has to ask the question, "What passion is there that is greater than my own?" People are known for different passions throughout history, people such as . . .

- Business innovators such as Henry Ford, Bill Gates, Fred Smith, and Mark Zuckerberg.

- Great athletes such as Michael Jordan, Marion Jones, and Mark McGwire.

- Creative geniuses such as Pablo Picasso, Buckminster Fuller, or Wolfgang Amadeus Mozart.

- Revolutionary thinkers such as Marie Curie, Thomas Edison, and Albert Einstein.

- Spiritual leaders such as John Wesley, Billy Graham and Mother Teresa.

They were successful in what they did because of a life filled with passion. Throughout my life I have met men and women who had passion for the work they did. Some were for others, and some were for their own glory. Two men grabbed my attention with their exemplary lives of passion. These men made great sacrifices for their calling to help people and persevered in order to see their passion realized.

Steve Park of Little Lights Urban Ministries

Over ten years ago, when I first met Steve, he didn't have a ministry name but served his community where his father had a business. The business was located in the inner cities of Washington DC. He told me what he was doing and how his heart was for the children who didn't have any support for academics. To be honest, at first I thought he was just joking. During that period there weren't many Asians, let alone Koreans, willing to spend their evenings helping inner city children. They would have to sacrifice the usual Asian goals for success and enable others to become successful. This was not what his parents dreamed for him.

But his heart was burdened to help the children and in 1994, while helping to run a day camp, Steve met Darrell, a junior high school boy who could not read. There the Lord convicted his heart even more. Moved by this friendship, Steve prayed about how to combine his desire to share God's love with helping children who were struggling in school. The Lord answered his prayer by giving him the vision to start an inner city ministry.

In 1995, Little Lights was born and began sharing God's love with underprivileged children and their families in Southeast Washington DC. Little Lights is truly an impacting and transforming ministry dedicated to serving the children and families of Potomac Gardens, one of the last remaining public housing complexes on Capitol Hill. Ninety percent of approximately 350 children ages 5-17 live in households headed by single moms, and it is estimated that without intervention less than 2% of the complex's youth will attend college.

How do I know that Steve has passion for this ministry? Steve and his wife, a few years after the inception of the ministry, moved to Southeast DC to be closer to the people they serve. Even after a decade the whole family, including their two children, still live there.

Most Asians, even if they were poor would not dare to take on that kind of challenge and move into a neighborhood that is known to be unsafe. But Steve had a passion to serve these children and had a brighter vision for the kids and their families. He is truly a man of passion with a willingness to live beyond his own comfort. God is truly blessing the ministry and after a decade of operation, his passion is still brightly glowing.

Little Lights Urban Ministries has been proportionately recognized for its efforts. Even the South Korean President's wife made a special visit to affirm its work in the inner city. But the effectiveness of his ministry and the service he provides is not the best part of what he does. Allowing Christ to continually transform him into Christ's image is Steve's biggest legacy. His growing passion is the evidence.

David Anderson of Bridgeway Community Church

As I look across the auditorium, I see people of many races, classes, and cultures: African American, Africans, Caucasians, Hispanics, Asians, and many others. Over 2,500 gather for Sunday morning services. If we could picture heaven the way it is described in the Bible (people from every nation all worshipping God together), Bridgeway Community Church would come close.

This stunning picture of a multiracial group praising and worshipping God was not painted overnight nor was it achieved without adversity. The vision from God was clear, but his passion for a multicultural ministry was soon met with many challenges, even from church consultants. David speaks plainly in his book _Multicultural Ministry_, _"There were many challenges along the way. Church planting has not been an easy route. However, hearing church consultants speak against multicultural ministry in the early 1990s actually inspired in me a greater desire to overcome the hurdles. For example, one consultant said, 'David, I have never seen a racially mixed church grow without one culture having to die. If there are blacks and whites in the church, then one of the cultures died within the church.'"_[5]

Planting a church is difficult, but planting a multicultural church is even more challenging because of the racial and cultural issues that are involved. However, in 1986 a young man had a inspiring vision to start an integrated church in the Washington DC area and to lead a multicultural army of Christ-followers, moving forward in unity and love. This is Bridgeway's vision.

Bill Hybels in his forward to _Multicultural Ministry_ writes, _"David Anderson invited me to speak at the tenth anniversary for Bridgeway Community Church. David had been an intern at Willow Creek and had demonstrated his leadership gift and love for the church during that time. Yet David's vision of the body of Christ was different."_ Hybels continues, _"His vision was of a multicultural church. He saw African-Americans, Caucasians, Koreans, Latinos, and Jewish believers all celebrating the grace of God, who created beautiful and amazing diversity within the human race. David saw not the suppression of diversity but the blending of cultures in praise to God."_[6]

Through years of difficulties and challenges, David never gave up on his passion to see a multicultural army of Christ followers now worshipping together every Sunday at Bridgeway Community Church. And Dr. David Anderson's vision has become a passion for many other pastors who are seeking his advice and counsel on planting a multicultural church.

What's in your Passion?

Understanding your passion will help determine whether you are a fit for a particular church's core values. Billy Graham has a passion for lost souls, and everyone who has heard about him can sense it: Billy Graham Schools of Evangelism, Billy Graham School of Missions and Evangelism, Billy Graham Evangelistic Association and more are all products of his passion.

People recognize Loren Cunningham's passion for missions. As the founder of Youth With A Mission (YWAM), he has traveled to every country on earth in order to impact people for Christ in some significant manner. Every full-time missionary with YWAM shows a similar passion to reach the lost for Christ. The organization chooses their missionaries based on their sense of the candidate's passion.

Everyone has different areas of passion. Michael Jordan has basketball, Tiger Woods has golf, Bill Gates has computer software, Billy Graham has evangelism, and John Maxwell has leadership. They are all driven by a cause either to win a game or to influence a life. Whether it's a passion for a game or influence, when Christ invades our lives, He plants a passion in our hearts so that we can be a transforming agent for God's kingdom. Every believer has a passion because each one of us has been given a spiritual gift. Our passion will encompass our gift so we don't have to look far to find it. First find your giftedness and your passion will not be too far away. If you are unsure of what your passion is, here are some determining guidelines:

1. Get to know Christ and His Word. It may sound like a cliché for believers who are already committed to ministry, but the reminder will keep you on the right track as you seek to streamline your service for the Lord. Let His heart impact yours. Find out what His passion is, and let it become yours.

2. Pray for conviction and then confirmation. You can be sure that if a passion is a match with who you are, your heart will tell you. You will not be able to stop it.

3. Patiently wait for God's passion to be revealed in you. One reason God takes long to reveal our passion is He wants to mature us to a certain degree before we serve in the area of our passion. Then He matures us while we're expressing the passion He gave us. Conforming us into the image of Christ is the goal in everything He does in our lives.

4. Recognize your passion by its longevity. Even after many hardships and trials that challenged your passion, it will not die or wane. It won't go away. God's call is irrevocable.

5. Recognize your passion by its potential. When God gives us a passion to serve Him, He will challenge us so that we will

rely on Him. He will challenge us to do more than we can do on our own. If we follow Him, we will have a greater influence than we can imagine.

6. Don't confuse your second or third passion with your first one. There will be competing passions that must take a back seat to your primary one. After you've determined or recognized your ultimate passion, don't get sidetracked by smaller ones.

Below are some questions and comments to ask yourself to determine your passion:

1. What joys in life have been consistent over the years? Even when things were difficult, you found joy in doing it. It brings a smile to your face when you think about doing it.

2. Though the work may be difficult for others, it may appear to be easy for you. They see that you love it. It may tire others, but it energizes you.

3. You're constantly thinking about it or talking about it. As a matter of fact if we recorded every word you say, we would be able to determine your passion by the subject you talk about the most. This is for those who are already expressing their passions. For those who haven't found it yet, it is still in their thoughts.

4. Is your pursuit all-consuming? Your primary passion will take over your life. It can be dangerous if not balanced. You can sacrifice your family and your health for it.

5. Has your service or pursuit seen some resurrections? When you failed in the area of your service, did it revive?

6. Am I willing to die for the sake of this cause?

People with passion always work hard. Even when they fail, they are motivated to press on. What may seem repetitive to others is a joy to the one who has that passion. Their work, career, and ministry bring them continued satisfaction. What was the passion of our Lord? He revealed it in John 4:34 *"My food,"* said Jesus *"is to do the will of him who sent me and to finish his work."* What energized Jesus was the will of His Father and the work He had called Jesus to do. Living for a paycheck is not life. Jesus doesn't want us to live for mere existence. He came to give us life and that more abundantly. He came to give us a passionate life (John 10:10).

> He came to give us a passionate life.
>
> John 10:10

Questions to Answer:

To the Hiring Church: What is your identity?

_____

_____

_____

_____

To the potential EM pastor: What is your passion?

_____

_____

_____

_____

Are we a match? Yes _____ No _____

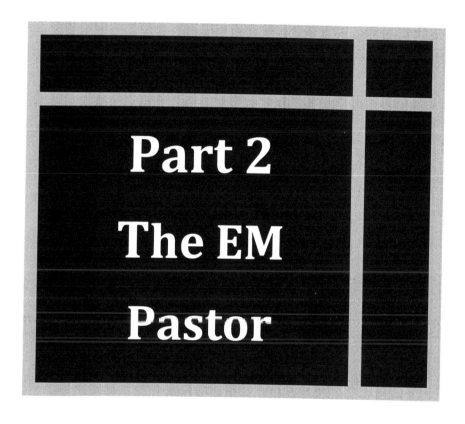

Part 2
The EM
Pastor

A careful evaluation of the job descriptions revealed problems in the search criteria. The expectations placed on the new EM pastor were not realistic. Failure was inevitable because most EM pastors have an aversion to the 1st gen Asian style of leadership. Although it is ideal to seek for both the leader and the shepherd, they may be two different people instead of being

2

The EM Pastor

embodied in one. In fact many seminary students who desire to become pastors learn how to preach and teach the Bible and not how to nurture and care for the sheep because the master of divinity program in many seminaries focuses primarily on interpreting the Bible as the core curriculum. Though some seminaries do offer masters or doctorate programs in pastoral counseling, many are not able to acquire two master-level degrees. Nurturing and shepherding skills are traditionally gained from other areas of life or from trial-and-error ministry experiences.

In the Pastoral Psychology journal a study was done by Jin Han and Cameron Lee to indentify four types of congregational intrusiveness that increase ministry demand and stress among Korean American pastors. The four primary areas are: personal criticism of the minister, the presumptive expectations of the minister's flexibility and availability, boundary ambiguity, and criticism of the minister's family.[7]

The authors conclude that boundary ambiguity and presumptive expectations are the most common stress factors for Korean American pastors. It is important to identify these stress factors so that those who are in leadership can create a work environment where the stresses of the culture will be reduced or greatly minimized.

> The authors reveal that the boundary ambiguity and presumptive expectations are the most common stress factors.

A constant level of stress will develop into a burnout and when burned out, problems seem insurmountable with everything looking bleak, and it is difficult to muster up the energy to care—let alone do something about the situation. The stress level and burnout can threaten a pastor's job and most importantly a drift in the relationship that has been developed over the years. However, burnout can be healed, reduced or avoided if you plan out a solid foundation of boundary from the beginning or inception of the ministry.

Chapter 4

Pastor Expectations

What are your expectations?

Boundary Ambiguity and Presumptive Expectations

Ambiguity in boundaries and misplaced hopes upon the EM pastor can start a conflict that was not necessary to begin with. Shortly after I began serving as a minister of a large multicultural church I realized that there was no young adults ministry, a typical ministry in many AsiAm churches. I chose ten young adults to come to our house for dinner, but before the invitation I sowed a seed in their minds about starting a brand new ministry at the church. With excitement all ten showed up. After dinner and a short prayer, I asked everyone what their hopes and expectations were concerning this new young adults ministry. Everyone expressed their excitement and expectations, thinking that it would be similar to the ones they enjoyed in their previous churches.

After everyone spoke I said, "It's great that everyone has these hopes and expectations expressed today, but I have to be honest with all of you; I will fail each of your expectations." Soon, everyone's face turned from joyful expressions to puzzlement–the "What in the world is he saying!?" look. I further explained, "I'm sure to fail all your expectations of this new ministry because my talent and skill alone will not be able to accomplish all that you desire. For one reason or another when I or someone else in our team fails, disappoint will settle in your hearts and germinate. These unmet expectations will ultimately lead to bad relationships because it will cause disunity. How? The one who was disappointed will distance himself from the one who caused the pain. One member has now broken off from the team. And, a broken team will result in a broken ministry. In the long run the ministry will not do well because of false hopes and expectations placed on the leader before the ministry began."

Since no one in the group was married, I explained the problems that married couples go through with expectations. "I know that no one here is married," I said "but, it has been my observation and the statistics on divorce clearly show that anyone getting married with the hope that his spouse will fulfill all his expectations (which are mostly unspoken), will soon come to a hard realization that they were unrealistic. At that point, many will seek marriage counseling but because the hurts ran deep and the conflicts hardened their hearts, they will separate for a time or divorce."

Several were still looking at me with confusion. I could hear what they were saying in their minds, "Okay, now what? How do we proceed from here?" Thankfully, before I brought them together I'd been in prayer for quite some time, seeking the Lord's guidance in this matter. The conviction was clear to set the foundation for the new young adults ministry and to direct their expectations toward Jesus who would guide them in all that they did. I have seen too many new ministries begin with excitement but end in disappointment after unmet expectations or the departure of its leadership. Too much hope was placed on the EM pastor and expectations of the KM leaders and EM congregation were not met, so disappointment led to a "divorce." The people forget that ministers are humans too, susceptible to failures just like everyone else.

South Korea has one of the highest teen suicide rates in the world. Rapid growth in the economy has changed the way South Koreans regard life. The internal value system has weakened and the country has become too materialistic and achievement oriented. Many young students cannot meet the expectations of their parents or their culture in academic achievement. Unfortunately, many choose suicide as the solution. But for those who do not choose to "end it all," what kind of life do they have?

Most KM pastors, elders, and other church leaders place unrealistic expectations on the EM pastors. Even on some EM leaders, superhuman expectations are placed that create unnecessary tension between them and the rest of the church body. Frustration and conflict can be avoided by clarifying the job description or ministry roles and discussing the unwritten expectations that the parties harbor.

Romans 3:22-24 (NASB)

[22] even the righteousness of God through faith in Jesus Christ for all those who believe; for there is no distinction; [23] for all have sinned and fall short of the glory of God, [24] being justified as a gift by His grace through the redemption which is in Christ Jesus;

All pastors *"fall short of the glory of God"* and will never meet the high expectations placed on them by the leadership of the church or the rest of the congregation. Failure is inevitable. Barna Research

Group, a premier Christian research firm, did a nationwide survey among 1,005 adults. Those who were surveyed identified things that were "very important" for a leader to do. According to the research data, the following profile was obtained:[8]

- 87% expect leaders to motivate people to get involved in meaningful causes and activity

- 78% believe leaders should negotiate compromises and resolve conflicts when they arise

- 77% look to leaders to determine and convey the course of action that people should take in order to produce desirable conditions and outcomes

- 76% rely on leaders to identify and implement courses of action that are in the best interests of society, even if some of those choices are unpopular

- 75% expect leaders to invest their time and energy in training more leaders who will help bring the vision to reality

- 63% want leaders to communicate vision so that they know where things are headed and what it will take to get there

- 61% say leaders are responsible for the direction and production of employees associated with the leader's organization or cause

- 61% think leaders should analyze situations and create the strategies and plans that direct the resources of those who follow them

- 56% hold leaders responsible for managing the day-to-day details of the operation

Barna reports that the list continues. The followers' additional expectations were: direct activity, encourage participants, supply resources, motivate participants, strategize, manage people, recruit, train and develop new leaders, resolve conflicts and more. Barna noted, *"We have been taught that leadership is about one individual performing all of an organization's critical tasks – motivating, mobilizing, directing, and resourcing people to fulfill a vision – at a level of excellence and influence that separates him or her from the bulk of humanity. The combination of skills and abilities required to be a great leader has caused many people to lament the absence of leaders in our society."* The author continues, *"Would you agree that a person would have to be superhuman to accomplish all of these tasks? Yet that's what we expect a leader to do. No wonder we are consistently disappointed by leaders who seemed to hold such promise before they assumed positions of significant authority and responsibility."*[9]

When it comes to expectations, even the Lord didn't meet the high standards of his disciples. Jesus couldn't bring the kingdom fast enough. Talking about His own demise was a disappointment to Peter (Matt 16:23). His brothers tried to dictate what He should do (John 7:3). And Satan was constantly on Jesus to prove Himself (Matt 4:1-11). If the Lord was a disappointment to His people and

He was perfect, how much will we fall short of the standards people set for us? Ministers are treated like "spiritual giants" who can leap over tall ministry obstacles with a single bound, who are faster than the trends that plague the church, and who are more powerful than the sum total of the sheep's prayers. He is expected to be the "super" shepherd.

I have seen and experienced firsthand what happens in the Christian community when high standards are placed upon leaders as if they are some type of "spiritual giants." Every leader fails to meet the expectations of his congregation members in one way or another. It is guaranteed that some members, leaders, elders, associate pastors, and even some visitors will not be satisfied with the sr. pastor's performance no matter how hard the minister tries.

This is where I learned the most important lesson: Always direct people to Jesus. One of the most valuable tools that I learned when praying for someone was to always end with prayer by connecting the person back to Christ. By connecting the person back to Christ, the person's dependence was not on the pastor but on the One who could do the impossible. Allowing God to determine the expectations gives the leader the freedom to move based on the Holy Spirit's guidance and not on whims of the congregation.

> By connecting the person back to Christ, the person's dependence was not on the pastor but on the One who could do the impossible.

With no high expectations for the pastor to be the "spiritual giant or superhuman," he can naturally apply his gifting and passion without the burdens to prove his leadership. The pastor now has room to listen to the Holy Spirit's guidance and move, guide, organize, strategize, and lead the congregation to what God has planned and willed.

Proverbs 16:9 (NIV)
In his heart a man plans his course,
but the LORD determines his steps.

Boundary of Expectation

So what expectations can be placed upon a pastor being hired by the church? Are all expectations wrong? Having a clear and concise explanation of the expectation of the pastor is helpful.

When churches just put the "wants" and "desires" of a pastor in the job category, it is similar to giving a child a jar of candy and telling the child to just eat one. The child has no understanding of the boundary he must have. Without an adult giving a child the specific boundary, the desires and the actions of the child could result in cavities and dental costs for the parents. Without a boundary of expectation of the job position, there could be a significant level of miscommunications and misunderstandings which contributes to the stress level for the church and the pastor.

As previously mentioned, Jin Han and Cameron Lee identified the greatest indicators of stress among Korean American pastors to be the boundary ambiguity and presumptive expectations. One of the ways to reduce ambiguity and expectations are to have a clear job description and expectations on paper before a potential EM/Youth pastor is interviewed. Unless the job is described and defined, people will not be able to work effectively. There is a high probability that conflict, boundary ambiguity, authority vagueness, and uncertain expectations will arise because of lack of clarity from the inception of the role explanation. It is essential for churches to have carefully developed job or position descriptions because clarity in job descriptions will help people in ministry to do an effective work and help the whole church fulfill God's call to ministry.

The following is an example from a church that understands the importance of setting a boundary and setting specific expectation as a road map for the pastor.

[**Sample:** This is not a job description but a specific section dedicated to "expectations" of the pastor. Further information and samples of job descriptions can be found in Part 5 Optional Hiring Methods and Appendix A]

Expectations

1. The Executive Pastor is to have a genuine relationship with Jesus Christ and is actively seek a deeper relationship with Him. This belief should be lived out in such a way that it is obvious to those in the leadership of (church name) and the church family.

2. The Executive Pastor is to be a team player of (church name).

3. The Executive Pastor will recognize that working with a team is essential to successful ministry. It is expected that he work closely

with other staff members and develop a support team of volunteers made up of Team Players.

4. The Executive Pastor will be disciplined and diligent with his time, keeping a balance between home and work.

5. The Executive Pastor is to spend time throughout the year developing his skills in ministry, developing his character, and sharpening his knowledge and understanding in ministering to people while fulfilling his role as executive pastor.

6. The elders in conjunction with the Senior Pastor will evaluate the Executive Pastor annually. The ministry staff will participate in annual evaluations of the Executive Pastor.

From the Heart of an EM Pastor

This book is excellent. I recently went through a horrible ordeal in applying for the youth director position at a Chinese church. I am bi-racial, second generation where Toishan Chinese was my first language until five years old. You are dead on about knowing the description and expectations for the position. I was asked to apply for the directorship, but they offered the associate youth position instead. I went in to the process being invited to apply for the directorship by two of the current pastors; the board went into the process believing they had three options to offer. The options were directorship, associate director, and internship. I did not know this was the situation, and it was never spoken about. The board needs to be clear about the position they are hiring for, and the applicant needs to ask for clarity of the position one is applying for.

One major mistake I made was to not to remember who my audience was when I preached. I was to preach to the youth, but in attendance were many parents. I preached as I would to any youth group. The feedback that I received was that I was not a strong speaker and that speaking on Sundays was the most important aspect as youth director because the majority of the youth only attended on Sundays. I should have preached as if I were preaching to the adults using the methods that they are used to hearing. The applicant needs to know what the most important requirement for the position is. Apparently preaching and speaking was the main skill the new director needed to be capable of performing.

I cannot even begin to reveal all of the hurtful things that occurred during this candidacy process, but because of this event, I cannot remain as a member of this church. Eventually, I left the part time employment to another Chinese church because of cultural differences and hurts caused by misunderstandings. I even thought about quitting ministry altogether.

You have a timely book for Asian churches.

Chapter 5

Responsibilities of the EM Pastor

Responsibilities include but are not
limited to . . .

Church members expect the pastor to be responsible with more things than he can handle. A youth pastor was rebuked by his First Generation Immigrant (FiGI) church leaders for not disciplining the kids. He responded to the elders that it was not his role to discipline their children, but to point them to Jesus. Not too long after this meeting, he was requested to leave. Surely the responsibility was misdirected to the youth pastor, but had the leadership team discussed this with him before the hiring process, this situation would not have occurred.

It is interesting to note when challenging the hiring committee to prioritize what they consider as the most important duties of a pastor, many prioritize based on how they feel. They look at the bad experiences from the previous pastor and favor the opposite. Possible list of duties include but are not limited to:

1. Administration
2. Spiritual or Christian education
3. Preaching / teaching

4. Sermon preparation
5. Promotion & marketing old & new ministry programs
6. Missions
7. Church discipline
8. Community service
9. Counseling
10. Evangelism
11. Prayer
12. Interpersonal skills or personal relations
13. Visitations (hospital/home/work, etc.)
14. Funerals
15. Weddings
16. Vision (planting/moving/growing)
17. Leadership
18. Revamping old and developing new and innovative programs
19. Spiritual formation (personal)
20. Mentoring
21. Family time
22. Other _____

I would encourage you to ask your hiring committee how many hours they expect the pastor to spend on each one. You will find the results to be staggering. There are many Christian resources on this subject. In general preaching and teaching typically score high, but sermon preparation score low or is given just a few hours. When this is the case, research indicates the leaders of the Hiring Church truly do not believe that preaching and teaching to be a high priority.

Christians believe that their pastor should have good administration skills, especially if they belong to small churches. However, they fail to recognize that not everyone has the same spiritual gifts and not everyone has administrative gifts. Many churches desire a pastor to have good interpersonal skills, remarkable preaching and biblical teaching expertise, excellent administrative gifts, and good counseling adeptness. They also have the unspoken expectation that he would run errands for the senior pastor as many EM/Youth pastors do.

Acts 6:2-4

2 So the Twelve gathered all the disciples together and said, "It would not be right for us to neglect the ministry of the word of God in order to wait on tables. 3 Brothers and sisters, choose seven men from among you who are known to be full of the Spirit and wisdom. We will turn this responsibility over to them 4 and will give our attention to prayer and the ministry of the word."

The disciples gathered together and agreed that *"It would not be right for us to neglect the ministry of the word of God in order to wait on tables."* It is interesting to note that the "twelve" are not condoning nor devaluing the importance of waiting on "tables" but focusing on the continuing the declaration of the "word of God" as their primary roles for the kingdom.

1 Timothy 5:16

If any woman who is a believer has widows in her care, she should continue to help them and not let the church be burdened with them, so that the church can help those widows who are really in need.

It is not that the church is unwilling to help the widows who have daughters or daughters-in-law. The emphasis is that family should take care of family unless that is not possible. Widows who are really in need are those who don't have families to take care of them. When we have capable servants who can manage the affairs of the church so that the minister can preach and teach the word effectively, we should not add those duties to the minister and weigh him down.

General biblical perspective of the pastor's role:

1. **Spiritual Leadership** John 21:16 - Jesus said, *"Take care of my sheep."* John 21:17 … Jesus said, *"Feed my sheep."*

2. **Oversight of the Church** Acts 20:28 - Keep watch over yourselves and all the flock of which the Holy Spirit has made you overseers. Be shepherds of the church of God, which he bought with his own blood.

3. **Shepherd the church** 1 Peter 5:2 - Be shepherds of God's flock that is under your care, watching over them—not because you must, but because you are willing, as God wants you to be; not pursuing dishonest gain, but eager to serve;

4. **Pray** Acts 6:4 - *"and will give our attention to prayer and the ministry of the word."* Ephesians 6:18 - And pray in the Spirit on all occasions with all kinds of prayers and requests. With

this in mind, be alert and always keep on praying for all the Lord's people.

5. **Preach and teach the Word** 1 Timothy 5:17 - The elders who direct the affairs of the church well are worthy of double honor, especially those whose work is preaching and teaching.

6. **Equip the saints** Ephesians 4:12 - to equip his people for works of service, so that the body of Christ may be built up.

7. **Love** John 13:34-35 *"A new command I give you: Love one another. As I have loved you, so you must love one another. By this everyone will know that you are my disciples, if you love one another."*

Chapter 6

Vision for EM

What is your vision for the English Ministry?

In analyzing the "responsibilities and duties" of the EM pastor, the general consensus is as follows:

Primary Responsibilities

1. Preaching / leading Sunday worship

2. Leading Bible studies

3. Developing, training, equipping, and discipling leaders

4. Developing EM vision and set goals

5. Planning programs and events (revivals, retreats, missions, small groups, etc.)

6. Spiritually nurturing and counseling / pastoral care

Most hiring churches want the EM pastor to develop a "vision" for the EM congregation. In researching this portion, I have found that it's a real issue to ask a newly hired or a potential EM pastor to formulate a "vision" for the English Ministry.

It's a real issue to ask a newly hired or a potential EM pastor to formulate a "vision" for the English Ministry.

From the Heart of an EM Pastor

At both of the search committee's and elder board's interview, I presented my plan and gave my vision for the youth group. I did not give copies to the parents. This caused the parents to state I did not have a vision.

During the telephone interview, one of the things he asked for me to prepare was a vision plan for the EM. I told them that I would prepare one for the EM and make it similar to the KM's vision. I asked them for their vision and mission statements. It was silent. He went to another question.

Wayne Cordeiro is the senior pastor of New Hope Christian Fellowship in Honolulu, Hawaii, one of the nation's fastest growing churches with over 10,000 in attendance on weekend services and 8,500 of those are new Christians. Pastor Cordeiro discusses his primary obstacle as the unity of a church. He notes, *"One of the main obstacles to unity is failing to identify what we are all about. Without a clear, concise vision that is understood by everyone, unity is compromised. And let me hasten to add: there is one thing worse than a ministry without vision. It is a ministry with too many visions! Those various visions will be seeds of dissent in your ministry."* [10]

Pastor Park was the newly hired EM pastor. The elder in charge of hiring process interviewed only a handful of candidates. Actually, he worked through a network of people he knew. Many of the 1st immigrant Korean and Chinese churches that I know usually hire through a network of people rather than choosing someone by patiently pouring over resumes. This is the reason why multi-level marketing and other network related businesses are one of the fastest growing and successful businesses throughout Asia. Asians advertise by word of mouth and prefer to do business relationally.

The elder contacted Pastor Park through one congregation member who had a relative who knew an EM pastor, who recommended another EM pastor who was looking for a position. Pastor Park was formerly a youth pastor but now wanted the experience and challenge of being a full-time EM pastor. During the interview he was asked, "What is your vision for the EM?" From his American seminary education along with his own personal experience of going through a Korean church split, he came up with a vision that sounded much like "corporate America" and looked well on paper. Everything looked and sounded good because of the listing of such words as "revival," "spiritual growth," "small groups," and "developing future leaders." The elder in charge had never been fully involved with the EM so as far as he was concerned everything sounded positive so he gave the recommendation to the KM pastor and hiring committee to hire him.

The KM pastor was not involved in the candidating process nor was he present when the EM pastor delivered his sermon during his visit. The college students and the few young adults in the EM did not fully understand what was truly going on with the Korean style of hiring an EM pastor. But everyone agreed that there was nothing to dislike about Pastor Park and since the number of applications coming in were very slim, the new candidate was hired.

Within a short period, Pastor Park looked to form a core team to grow the EM as outlined in his vision for the EM. However, he did not realize that a small percentage of people who were heavily involved in the church when they were pastorless now needed a break. This faithful group was ready to step down because they were burnt out. Relieved to have the new pastor take up the load, they were no longer available to serve.

Pastor Park was not aware of this pattern in a church, so his plan began to unravel. Whatever the situation may be, whenever a prominent congregation member leaves or steps down, the blame is automatically placed on the new EM pastor. The congregation members who had planned to step down for a while never expressed their intentions. Negative communication is rarely practiced in an Asian church. In fact it's not a cultural thing to do.

Pastor Park continued his plan and eventually found a small but growing number of people willing to follow the new vision. Meetings were set to disciple and grow the small leadership team. However, one major problem stood in his way. Most of the core team members were also involved with the children and youth ministries. Since these teachers spoke English well, the KM relied heavily on them. That made it hard for them to break free to serve in the EM. And because the children's department had their own meetings and the part-time youth pastor had his own meetings, the volunteers would be strained even more trying to serve both ministries. And asking the volunteers to choose between serving in their present ministries and serving in the un-established new one wasn't something the new pastor was comfortable doing. The EM pastor had an uphill battle coming into a situation where the chips were stacked against his success.

The new EM pastor had many unexpected obstacles to work through. The core team explained that they would like to take part in the new EM team meeting, but they were already over-extended. Pastor Park was frustrated but he wasn't about to abandon his calling to be an EM pastor. He had a solid "vision" for the EM and was convinced that he could pull it off. And his persistence paid off because eventually the diligent servants stepped down from the children's and youth ministries to become part of the core team of the English Ministry. Unfortunately, this did not sit well with the KM pastor and leadership. Complaints came in from some of the 1st gen congregation members who had to step up to teach. They were indirectly forced to volunteer because there were no others. They felt that they could not speak English well enough to communicate with the children. The complaints reached the elders and the KM pastor. In the beginning the KM pastor and the elders were very supportive of the 2nd gen pastor's vision and goals, but when it started to interfere with the KM's programs, people, and facility, the vision of the EM pastor needed to take a back seat or stopped all together. The KM pastor and other leaders who were not involved with the EM were starting to show their displeasure of EM's direction. And because of the lack of communication between the KM and the EM pastors, several other issues were starting to surface. Usually when conflicts increase, dialog between the two ministries dwindle, leading to even more frustration. If these issues are left unresolved, the EM pastor's departure is inevitable. And that is what happened. By the third year Pastor Park decided to leave for another church, having learned what not to do from this experience.

Pastor Park's story exemplifies what happens when a potential EM pastor is asked at an interview, "What is your 'vision' for EM?"

> Asking the EM pastor to set a "vision" for the English Ministry results in a vision that clashes with the direction of the KM.

Asking the EM pastor to set a "vision" for the English Ministry results in a vision that clashes with the direction of the KM. Why is that? **KM already has a vision.** It's like asking a child what he wants to be when he grows up and telling him he can't be that because the parent has chosen a career for him already. Why bother asking then? It is best to let the candidate know what the church wants in an EM ministry and ask if he will support it. This is vital to the long-term relationship and the success of the KM and EM.

Some Korean churches realize the importance of this principle and mention it in the responsibility section of the job requirements, statements like: "Achieve our vision," "Implement our goals," "Work towards our vision," "Must be willing to follow the church's stated vision plan." These churches understand what happens when an EM has a different set of "vision plans" than the KM. They're trying to avoid the same problem by verbalizing their requirements.

In some situations when the church leaders are asking the EM pastor to set a vision for EM, they are actually asking, "How can you keep our kids busy doing church programs?" This is not the case with all the churches, but many of the KM leadership are so busy with their own ministry, they need someone to take care of their children and are not necessarily pursuing a growing EM. For those types of churches it is best to find someone to nurture, counsel, and shepherd the English Ministry than to have someone to lead and grow the congregation. In other words any KM looking to primarily build their own ministry needs a supply of volunteers and teachers which they expect the EM to provide. If the EM grows to the point where all the teachers and volunteers are needed in the EM, the KM will be left wanting. This is not what the KM wants and they will oppose it.

I was speaking with a 1st gen Korean pastor who was the senior pastor for seven years of a medium size church of approximately 500 members. During his time of service he had a stroke and a heart attack. The hospitalization was due to the amount of pressure he faced to grow the church: spiritually, numerically, and financially. The stress was caused by differing visions, the church had one and the pastor had another. After an encounter with God, he was convicted to change the direction of the church, but the elders and leaders of the church did not want the change. While the church was demanding from the pastor their goals and aspirations, the heart of the pastor was trying to implement a different set of priorities. Eventually, the clash separated the two visions and the pastor resigned. Now he travels to South Korea holding revivals in churches that have visions similar to his. Through these revivals, hundreds of people have accepted Christ. If differing visions separate those in the same generation, how much more will it separate those in different generations?

Different Visions Under One Umbrella

Exceptional Asian churches are willing to let EM pastors have their own vision. A good friend of mine is an EM pastor at a large Korean American church. His EM has steadily grown from 70 to close to 120 in less than two years. There are a few factors that clearly show the reason for his success.

1. First and foremost, the EM pastor is willing to be under the authority of the 1st gen KM leadership.

2. His vision is similar to the KM's overarching goal and vision.

3. He participates in many of the KM's strategy sessions and attends every early morning, prayer meeting at 5:30 am. He is not required to but does so to show unity in the body.

4. He communicates to the KM leadership in English, though tries his best effort in Korean. Although not everyone understands his Korean, the KM leaders can read English and comprehend what he says by facial expressions, tones, and body language.

5. The KM leaders appreciate the effort and willingness of the EM pastor to establish a good relationship.

6. He is content and happy where he is, even in his second year of service there. (Typically, it is in the second year that complaints start to arise in the EM pastor.)

Although slightly different than the KM's, the EM vision is consistent with the KM's when it comes to missions and evangelism as the overarching goals of the church. Similar visions create harmony and momentum. Differing visions in the two ministries will lead to division. Generally, in the Korean church context when the new EM pastor sets a vision and bears fruit, it's because the majority of the EM congregation does not serve in any other ministry and is able to dedicate its time and energy to the new vision.

Most people don't realize that vision and mission statements are very powerful. The application of the vision and mission gives direction and momentum and charts the course for the ministry toward its destination. Vision describes the long term objectives of the ministry and the mission specifies what the day to day activities should be, the short-terms goals of the ministry. The statement will clearly define and dictate the direction of all church programs such as revivals, retreats, missions, outreach, small groups, and many other programs. This is the reason why careful prayer and thought has to go into having a separate EM vision.

Understandably Pastor Park was moving his EM into a different direction than the KM because his vision was different. One of KM's visions was to spread the gospel through missions but

Pastor Park wanted to reach out to his local community. While the KM was thinking that missions was abroad, EM was thinking that missions included the neighborhood. KM's mindset did not want to deal with the cultural difference in the neighborhood, but wanted to be homogeneous or stay within their comfort zone. EM was thinking that we need to be interracial and multicultural, something the first gen has been resisting for years. In order to implement this new vision for EM, Pastor Park needed energy, time, resources, and finances. The plan was to reach his community consisting of many racial groups. Pastor Park's new vision of community outreach created a panic of opposition from the KM side. The KM mission coordinator kept bothering the KM pastor to find out why the EM no longer participated in the summer mission trips. Differing visions paved divergent paths for the 2 ministries.

Setting the Basic Vision

If your church does not have a vision, mission, core values, and strategies to fulfill the mission, use the following definitions formulate them:

- **Vision** is the desire or intended future result of your organization. The vision statement states what the ministry or church desires to become. The statement focuses on the desired path to the future as it becomes the source of inspiration and the decision-making process. The vision should explain why it is important to achieve the mission of the organization. The vision statement should define the overarching goal or purpose. The vision statement answers the question: "Where do we desire to go as a team?"

- **Mission** is what the church will achieve. This statement provides a path to realize the vision in line with its values. This statement further explains the fundamental purpose of the ministry which determines the critical processes and the desired level of service.

- **Core Value(s):** The core values are beliefs that are shared among the church body that drives the organization's culture, priorities, and pursuits.

- **Strategy** is a focused plan of action to achieve the desired goals of the organization. It also sets the policies or methods by which the goals are achieved.

(See appendix D for samples of each category)

If the current ministry or church does not have a vision and mission statements, core values, and strategies, then apply the 3Ps of ministry effectiveness: Pray – Plan – Proceed. During the time I was operating my own martial arts business of 350 customers and 15 instructors, I applied the simple method of the 3Ps to create my vision and mission statements as well as my core values and strategies.

Proverbs 16:3
Commit to the LORD whatever you do,
and your plans will succeed.

1. **Pray**: Praying and seeking God's wisdom and discernment about the specifics of the church vision and mission is vital. When starting a ministry, it is recommended that you first research the subject in books or on the internet. Then seek some advice from veterans in the ministry. Afterwards, take what you've found to the Lord for His final approval. Ask the Lord for clarity for the direction He wants you to go.

2. **Plan**: How will you complete your mission? Find the method you will use to achieve your goals. Plan thoroughly and corporately. The more the core team takes ownership of the mission, the more perseverance they will have when times get tough. Be open to God to change your plans.

Proverbs 16:9

In his heart a man plans his course,
but the LORD determines his steps.

3. **Proceed**: Constantly checking the progress of the journey with the Lord is essential to the health of the organization, ministry, and leaders. Obstacles and conflicts will arise, but allowing the Holy Spirit to check the progress of the mission will strengthen the hearts of the leaders. Give God the glory at every stage of the journey, putting the success of the ministry in His hands.

Chapter 7

Nehemiah's Call: Pray, Plan and Proceed

Let's see how the most successful civil engineer did it.

The Call / Vision / Passion

Nehemiah 1:1-2
¹ *The words of Nehemiah son of Hakaliah:*
In the month of Kislev in the twentieth year, while I was in the citadel of Susa, ² *Hanani, one of my brothers, came from Judah with some other men, and I questioned them about the Jewish remnant that had survived the exile, and also about Jerusalem.*

Nehemiah must have been thinking about his people who survived the exile as well as the city of Jerusalem for some time because he is the one who first asked the question concerning these matters. " . . . *I questioned them about the Jewish remnant that survived the exile, and also about Jerusalem" (v 2).* Upon hearing about their distress *"he sat down and wept" (v 4).* Because Nehemiah was so excited to see his brothers come back from Judah, he must have rushed to meet them, but after hearing the tragic news, he was no longer able to hold the burden inside. Whether you describe it a calling, vision, or just simply a burning passion to help the Jewish remnant and the holy

city, his heart was burdened. It is very easy to spot the passion in
Nehemiah from his prayer (vv 5–11).

Nehemiah 1:3-4

³ *They said to me, "Those who survived the exile and are back in the
province are in great trouble and disgrace. The wall of Jerusalem is broken
down, and its gates have been burned with fire."*
⁴ *When I heard these things, I sat down and wept. For some days I
mourned and fasted and prayed before the God of heaven.*

The Prayer

When Nehemiah heard one of his brothers from Judah about the
Jewish remnant that survived the exile and the state of Jerusalem,
his heart was crushed. The cupbearer could not hold back the tears
or the passion that was aroused in him. A fire was kindled in his
heart which compelled him to seek a solution from *"the great and
awesome God, who keeps his covenant of love"* to those who have been
faithful and *"obey his commands" (v 5).*

Nehemiah 1:11

¹¹ *Lord, let your ear be attentive to the prayer of this your servant and to
the prayer of your servants who delight in revering your name. Give your
servant success today by granting him favor in the presence of this man."*

The Plan

Why was Nehemiah asking God to grant him success? What plan
was he forging in his mind? How would he obtain favor from his
king? Was he "crazy" in thinking that King Artaxerxes of the entire

Persian Empire was simply going to grant him whatever he wanted? Had he forgotten the Scriptures concerning the cupbearer and the baker?

Genesis 40:1-3

¹ Some time later, the cupbearer and the baker of the king of Egypt offended their master, the king of Egypt. ² Pharaoh was angry with his two officials, the chief cupbearer and the chief baker, ³ and put them in custody in the house of the captain of the guard, in the same prison where Joseph was confined.

Nehemiah fasted and prayed for days as indicated in verse 4. During these days he was making plans to rebuild Jerusalem while waiting patiently for the Lord to lead him to approach the king. When the time came, Nehemiah pleaded, *"Give your servant success today by granting him favor in the presence of this man."* Artaxerxes was not the king. God was. Arty was just a man whose heart lied in the hand of God. Nehemiah must have sought God's wisdom and discernment for the details of his plan because after the king gave him a favorable response, he brought out his request. It took four months from Kislev when Nehemiah first heard the news (1:1) to Nisan when he was asked by the King. I believe God allowed for this time period so Nehemiah could think through the details of his mission and strategy to rebuild Jerusalem.

Nehemiah 2:6

⁶ Then the king, with the queen sitting beside him, asked me, "How long will your journey take, and when will you get back?" It pleased the king to send me; so I set a time.

When the king questioned the sadness on Nehemiah's face, Nehemiah was so afraid that he shouted, *"May the king live forever!"(2:2)*. I'm not sure if any cupbearer would have had the courage to speak, let alone shout. I am surprised that he didn't get thrown in jail like the other cupbearer in Joseph's story. But this was the day of Nehemiah's favor. God was in charge.

What is interesting is that Nehemiah did not rashly blurt out his request. He waited for God's timing and it was the king who first spoke and asked *"Why does your face look so sad when you are not ill? This can be nothing but sadness of heart"* (v 2). It is astonishing that a busy king would even recognize the emotions of his servant and be moved to ask this question. Talk about favor and the hand of God.

How do we know that Nehemiah had been thinking of a strategic plan?

A difficult question like "How long will your journey take, and when will you get back?" cannot be answered without a clear, thought-out plan. "I don't know. Let me think about it," would have been disrespectful. Nehemiah answered:

Nehemiah 2:7-8
[7] I also said to him, "If it pleases the king, may I have letters to the governors of Trans-Euphrates, so that they will provide me safe-conduct until I arrive in Judah? [8] And may I have a letter to Asaph, keeper of the royal park, so he will give me timber to make beams for the gates of the citadel by the temple and for the city wall and for the residence I will occupy?" And because the gracious hand of my God was on me, the king granted my requests.

How could a cupbearer come up with such a strategic plan of action? He didn't even think about the answer. He just blurted it out as if he had been planning and rehearsing this for months. He was neither an ambassador nor a general, yet he spoke with authority and conviction so his plan of action was given the green light. His passion to help the Jewish remnant and have the holy city rebuilt was realized because he had a plan. All this came from the mouth of a waiter.

Proceed

Many good EM pastors struggle the most in the "proceed" section of their ministry career. The cause was right and the passion was there, but when conflicts arose, they gave up on the church because they didn't know how to handle these issues. A good friend from California called me about an issue he was having with another lay leader. He was complaining that the EM pastor wasn't stepping up to help with this matter, and he also felt the EM pastor was trying to avoid the whole situation. He felt he needed to take action before things escalated. It was like Nehemiah's situation. Things were going smoothly until the enemy started firing missiles to stop the advancement of the project.

Nehemiah 6:2-3

²*Sanballat and Geshem sent to me, saying, "Come and let us meet together at Hakkephirim in the plain of Ono." But they intended to do me harm.*
³*And I sent messengers to them, saying, "I am doing a great work and I cannot come down. Why should the work stop while I leave it and come down to you?"*

How did Nehemiah recognize the invitation as a trap? Nehemiah gave a sharp reply to a reasonable invitation, because he was quick to discern the insincerity of his enemies. Nehemiah refused to be distracted by matters that would divert his energy and attention from his calling to rebuild Jerusalem's broken wall. When you're in the proceeding stage, the enemies will constantly attack: *"Four times they sent me the same message, and each time I gave them the same answer" (v 4).*

How could a cupbearer who didn't have military training nor foreign policy experience discern the enemy's motive? The answer is simple. Nehemiah focused on the priority of his mission and the call of God, and the Lord gave his servant abundant wisdom, discernment, and knowledge. Nehemiah did not deviate from the plan he received from the Lord.

- Nehemiah received a calling and was given a passion to follow it.

- Nehemiah had a mission and completed it with a strategic plan.

- Nehemiah was a cupbearer but was transformed into a general, mason, architect, carpenter, and diplomat.

Chapter 8

Qualifications

Qualifications for the EM Pastor
position are . . .

The consensus on the "qualifications" of the EM pastor is:

Qualifications

1. Master of Divinity degree

2. Fluency in English / able to speak Korean a plus

3. Previous experience in a Korean church a plus

4. Married

5. Strong calling to a Korean church

6. Strong conviction of God's calling

7. Strong commitment to the ministry

8. Denominational ordination or plan to be

Generally, KM pastors feel that EM pastors do not understand sacrificial service as much as they do. KM pastors dedicate much of their energy, time, and finances to grow the church, even if it means helping a church member with his visa, driver's license, search for a business, and his day in court. First gen pastors have made numerous sacrifices for the sake of their members.

Many years ago when immigration to the U.S. was much easier, Koreans came in droves within a short period of time. Koreans arrived in the U.S. in three waves. The first wave of Koreans immigrated in 1903 in order to work as low-wage laborers in Hawaii's sugar plantations. It began with a few hundred men, women, and children. Within a few years over 7,000 Koreans came in, mostly men looking to work in the famed sugar plantations.

Peter Hyun in his book _Man Sei!_ recounts the arrival of his parents to a Hawaiian sugar plantation:

> _Father and Mother arrived in Honolulu in February 1903; they were one of only five married couples among the one hundred and twenty Korean immigrants. Immediately upon arrival, they were taken to a sugar plantation and ordered to report for work the very next day. They worked ten hours a day, six days a week, and each received sixteen dollars a month. Father, as an overseer and interpreter, received thirty dollars a month. While looking after all the needs of the immigrant workers, Father organized a "Self-Rule Association" to help preserve their cultural identity as Koreans. In the evening, after work, he conducted classes in English for the workers. The news of his activities attracted many Korean laborers from other areas, and soon the Methodist Church in Honolulu invited Father to work for them._
>
> _He formally joined the Methodist Church and was assigned to look after all the Korean churches in the outlying areas. Now his family grew with the birth of his second daughter, Sister Elizabeth, in Honolulu. Big sister Alice had been born on the sugar_

plantation of Waipahu the year before. In recognition of his leadership, the Methodist Mission appointed Father to be the preacher for all the Koreans on the island of Kauai, the "Garden Island." There, traveling on horseback, he covered the island from one end to the other, taking care of the sick, arranging schooling for the children, and conducting religious services. His sermons never failed to combine Christian faith with Korean aspirations for national freedom. Recognizing his value, some of the plantation owners began making regular financial contributions. Among them, the Wilcoxes and the Isenbergs became not only staunch supporters but also lifetime friends. With their help, Father built the first Korean church on Kauai; it was situated on top of a hill near the town of Lihue [11]

Spurred on by the Korean War (which took place between 1950-1953) the next wave of immigrants came from 1950 to 1964. Many of the new arrivals were brides of U.S. servicemen, who fought in the Korean War. In 1952 the McCarran-Walter Act allowed Asians to immigrate in small numbers and allowed them to become U.S. citizens.

The third wave of Korean immigrants was considered the largest, and it began in 1965. My family arrived during this wave in the hot summer of 1975. Not too long after our arrival, we looked to Korean churches for community support, networking, and cultural gatherings. A small church community accepted us with open arms even though our family was not Christian. This is one of the reasons why the church became the hub of the Korean community. It was a familiar and welcoming community.

The second reason the Korean church became a hub of the Korean community is it continued the cultural experience. When Koreans got together, they ate Korean food, spoke Korean, and talked about Korean values and Korea in general. And because most Asians have a very hard work ethic, it was normal for a family to be working 12 to 14 hours a day, 6 days a week. So they looked forward to "Social Sunday" which was the only day they had to connect with friends and enjoy leisure. And since their day was filled with dealing with English speaking colleagues or customers in their broken English, it was a weekly respite to go to church and enjoy their comfortable culture.

The third reason the church became a hub of the Korean community is the networking. Where would a Korean who didn't speak English very well go to get advise on business ventures, to borrow money, or find a life partner? Naturally, he would go to Korea. But since it was half way around the world, they would go to the next best place which is "little" Korea - the church. And because the church was the center of the Korean community, it stands to reason that the church leader, the pastor, would be the center of it all. This is the experience of the 1st gen pastor. So what does an EM pastor have on his resume? How could an EM pastor even come close to appreciating the service the 1st gen pastor rendered?

One of my friends became an EM pastor for a church in South Korea. He was expected to show up early in the morning when the senior pastor arrived and was allowed to leave when the senior pastor left. In some cases the senior pastor would arrive as early as 6 a.m. and would not leave until 10 p.m. Eventually, this took a toll on his family, and he soon left the church. For my friend spending time with his family was very important, but for KM pastors, it was the call of duty to sacrifice their family in service to the church.

Context of Sacrifice and Service for EM Pastors

Like Peter Hyun's father, many 1st immigrant pastors serve tirelessly. This trend continues even if the church isn't an immigrant church. The first generation mentality has not changed much even after the church dynamics have changed. Their work ethic remains consistent. KM pastors sacrifice their time and energy in order serve the church, even if it means their own family suffers while sacrifice for the EM pastor can mean putting Jesus first and disappointing the church. In contrast the 2nd gen EM pastors view the traditional, sacrificial service to the church as detrimental rather than admirable. To some degree the ministry the KM pastors rendered was necessary for their time and situation; however, that is not the case for the EM pastors. The EM pastor's sacrifice comes in the form of giving up lucrative careers for the ministry. Rather than pursuing personal gains of fame and prestige, they lead by example by not compromising and facing the criticism. Instead of thinking they have to do whatever it takes to serve the body, they want to do the right thing. And keeping a balance between ministry and family is the right thing for the EM pastors.

> Instead of thinking they have to do whatever it takes to serve the body, they want to do the right thing. And keeping a balance between ministry and family is the right thing.

Furthermore, if an EM pastor is asked to sacrifice his family for the church, he will eventually leave that ministry to find another one. He may choose to serve only part-time or leave the KM ministry altogether in order to give more time to his family. Because the mindset of the EM pastor doesn't agree with the KM pastor's, the EM pastor is considered less devoted to the Lord. But in reality the devotion is not less, but different.

Chapter 9

Strong Calling

Are you called to this church?

Because the average length of service at a church for an EM pastor and the youth pastor is 3 years and 2.5 years respectively, many churches are starting to ask for a "strong calling or conviction." Churches are looking for a greater commitment of length of term and loyalty.

As the erosion rate increases church leaders are asking for greater commitment from those who will serve at their church. They are making sure that the request is included in the job requirements. One thing is described three different ways:

- Strong calling in an Asian church context
- Strong conviction of God's calling
- Strong commitment to the ministry

In all three ways the churches are asking whether the candidate has staying power. The use of the word "strong" suggests that if the potential candidate only has an inclination in the areas mentioned, he may abandon ship when times get tough. The churches are trying to illuminate the transient ministers so that the congregation is spared the pain of starting a relationship that only lasts a short time, and the search committee doesn't have to go through the process every 3 years.

Are you called to this church?

The problem is best solved by asking the potential pastor, "Are you called to this church?" If the pastor has studied the church's vision, mission, core values, and strategy, then it is possible that the Holy Spirit has convicted the pastor that he is called to that church because the passion of the pastor matched the identity of the church. It is strongly encouraged that the church invite the pastor and his family to stay and fellowship with the congregation and church leaders for a full week, especially if the church is looking for a lead or senior pastor. The EM pastor's wife should be included in the process since she must support the move of her husband. In some denomination, the wife might be evaluated for her maturity since the requirement of an elder's wife is that she be a woman of exemplary character.

After the pastor and the church leaders have sought the Lord's guidance, everyone can come together to express his conviction, and if both parties confirm the match, it is then best to set a commitment time frame. Then, the desire of the church to have a "strong" commitment will be met by both the candidate and the hiring church.

I received a phone call from North Carolina and didn't realize that the KM pastor was interviewing me over the phone. My pastor friend called to let me know that a pastor from another state was going to call to ask some general questions. I had no idea that it was a phone interview. Since good EM pastors are hard to find, some 1st gen Asian pastors get pretty aggressive in their approach to hiring someone.

Basically he asked if I would be interested in coming to his fast-growing church. They were in desperate need of help, and he thought I would be the perfect candidate. He called me during the time I had lost everything including my business that I built up for over ten years and our nice big house. A former employee who had a gambling addiction stole my business checks and embezzled all my money. I was bankrupt and lost my business, house, cars, and other assets.

With a negative balance in my bank account and no food to feed my wife and three children, I was tempted to accept the offer from this church. I said "tempted" because I wasn't sure if this is where God wanted me to go. The good salary including full health benefits for the whole household was definitely something to consider. I asked the pastor if he could wait two weeks for us to pray and consider his offer. He agreed. During prayer and fasting, both my wife and I did not feel led to his church. The offer was good, especially in our time of need, but the Spirit's conviction gave us peace to just stay. I called the pastor and declined the offer. He didn't like it, but I had to be obedient to God.

This was one of the most difficult times of our lives. We were not sure where God was leading us. And, when you don't have the finances to support your own family, turning down a job offer is much more difficult. In fact I had two more offers and both were from a different part of the country. Each time my wife and I fasted and prayed, seeking the Lord's direction to see if we were called to ˙ ˉᵓ churches. But we didn't have peace about going to those ⁞ declined the offers. Also note that my wife and I made the decision together. She knew we were going to suffer for it, but we were united in the decision. The Lord was truly leading us.

An offer came in from a multicultural church. My wife and I fasted and prayed. Even though the offer was for a part-time position, when my wife and I prayed about it, the Lord convicted us to go to this church. The offer wasn't even made yet, but the calling was clear. However, I didn't want to just go in obedience only, I wanted to know what God's purpose for me was at this church. The Lord gave me that purpose, and so I accepted the offer with my wife's approval.

Knowing why is a privilege that children of God have. Jesus tells his disciples that everything he received from the Father, he has made known to them. While a servant doesn't know his master's business, a son should, and God will reveal the purpose for which we are sent to a particular place, especially if it is for long term.

John 15:15

I no longer call you servants, because a servant does not know his master's business. Instead, I have called you friends, for everything that I learned from my Father I have made known to you.

Knowing why will give you staying power. When difficulty comes and we know we are called, we will work through it. If we don't know why we're there, we can bolt whenever we find it convenient. Consider service to the church as something between a job and a marriage. It is more than a job but less than a marriage. Unlike a marriage, a pastoral position is not until death do us part, but more than a job we don't relocate every time a better offer comes along.

The blessing of God marks those who have been obedient until the service at a church is complete. You will be able to leave with dignity and blessing rather than bitterness and resentment and the church's feelings will be mutual.

Understanding Your Calling

Called to Faith

Not everyone is "called" to be a full-time minister, but everyone is "called" to the faith. Every believer has experienced a call to faith when the challenge came to trust in the Lord Jesus in order to become a member of God's family. From every walk of life we were called to join His kingdom.

1 Timothy 6:12
12Fight the good fight of the faith. Take hold of the eternal life to which you were called and about which you made the good confession in the presence of many witnesses.

Called to Minister

After we join His family, God gives us some duties. We are called to minister to one another. Every believer is called to minister to other believers using their God-given gifts. However, there is a big difference between a "call to minister" and a "call into the ministry."

Ephesians 3:7
7 Of this gospel I was made a minister according to the gift of God's grace, which was given me by the working of his power.

Called into the Ministry

Throughout the Bible, God called or chose certain people for specific purposes. A call "into" the ministry is God's invitation to be set apart for the purpose of primarily serving His people. If you think you have been "called into the ministry," dedicate yourself to prayer, find Scriptural support, get confirmation from wise counsel, and make sure your spouse agrees with you. At first try to refuse. If you are really called, God will convince you even if you try to run away from His plan.

For every move toward ministry, I made sure that my wife was in agreement with me. When God first convicted me to attend seminary, I asked my wife for her opinion and prayer support. At first, my wife disagreed with me about attending seminary, so I waited for God to move her heart. A week later, the Lord moved my wife's heart and I started seminary. When churches asked me to serve in their ministry, I made sure that my wife was in agreement with me to serve those ministries. If you are married, get the full support of your wife, for without it the ministry will be divided, your prayers will be hindered, and you will lose endurance. If you are truly called by God, He will make a way for you to enter into the ministry by all the right means. He won't take any shortcuts to get you there.

Questions to Answer:

Based on this book, do you believe that you have too many expectations of the EM pastor / youth pastor / _____?
Yes_____ No_____ Other _____

Please explain your answer. [Check this portion with the other members of the hiring committee]

_____

_____

_____

_____

_____

If you were to choose three primary responsibilities for the pastor, what would they be and why?

1. _____

2. _____

3. _____

Please explain your reason for choosing these three.

_____

_____

_____

_____

Does your church have a vision? Yes_____ No_____

If "yes" than what are your vision, mission, and core values? If "no" then please write what you think they should be.

Vision:

_____

_____

_____

Mission:

_____

_____

_____

Core Value(s):

_____

_____

_____

_____

Question to the candidate:

"Are you called **into the ministry**?" If "yes" then how were you confirmed?

_____

_____

_____

_____

"Are you called to this church?" If "yes" then explain:

_____

_____

_____

_____

_____

What do you feel are your greatest strengths? Please mark only ten starting with the greatest at 1 to 10.

_____Administration

_____Spiritual or Christian education

_____Preaching / teaching

_____Promotion & marketing old/new ministry programs

_____Missions

_____Church discipline

_____Community service

_____Counseling

_____Evangelism

_____Prayer

_____Sermon preparation

_____Interpersonal skills or personal relations

_____Visitations (hospital/home/work, etc.)

_____Funerals

_____Weddings

_____Vision (planting/moving/growing)

_____Leadership

_____Revamping old and developing new and innovative programs

_____Spiritual formation

_____Mentoring

_____Family time

_____Other _____

_____Other _____

Part 3

Merging of the Benefits

A small but growing Korean American church was in need of help with its youth to college students. Information was sent to the nearest seminary to recruit any Korean American student for aid. They couldn't afford to offer a full-time position so they advertised for a part-time help.

3
Merging of the Benefits

Pastor Jung was paying for his seminary education by working part-time at the seminary and part-time at a nearby business. He had a wife and two children and was desperately trying to make ends meet. He had been approached before about helping out a local Korean church, but since his prior experience with working with the 1st gen leaders wasn't too good, he declined the offer. But this time it was different. With a growing family, his bills were piling up and he needed more financial options.

Pastor Jung wanted to have children after seminary but God had a different plan. Now money played a role in his decision to help the Korean church, and his wife agreed. The lay leader that was in charge of finding a pastor verbally explained the desires of the church and what they wanted to accomplish for the growing youth and college groups. Pastor Jung then met with the KM pastor and the lay leader over lunch, and they agreed that he would begin working as a part-time EM pastor. Similar to most Asian churches, everything was done verbally. There was nothing in writing to constitute an actual hire. The church accounting department decided to allocate his salary as a missions' expense to not complicate the tax reports.

His schedule at church seemed simple: working Friday evenings leading a Bible study and small groups, conducting Sunday worship, setting up retreats, planning and coordinating for summer short term mission trips, and counseling when needed. Staff meetings were once a week with the KM pastor and volunteers. Occasionally, Pastor Jung was requested to do other things besides the original agreement. The pay was $1,500 for part-time work without any health benefits.

Chapter 10

Part-time EM/Youth Pastor

Part-time responsibilities for the
EM/Youth pastor are . . .

This is an ad from California: "Our current pastor will be finishing seminary and will be moving away, thus the need for a pastor."

Part-time Responsibility

Note: The job descriptions for youth pastors and EM pastors were similar so they were combined and assimilated into one list.

The part-time responsibilities are:

1. Preaching / leading Sunday worship

2. Leading Bible studies / small groups

3. Training and developing leaders

4. Working with pastoral staff

5. Pastoral care / counseling

6. Shepherding / Spiritual leadership and direction

7. Planning / coordination / activities and events

8. Motivating congregation to serve

9. Committed leadership to EM

10. Willing to support vision

The responsibilities of an EM pastor working part-time were very similar to those of a pastor working full-time. There were not many differences between the two diverse job positions. In fact in some cases there were more responsibilities for a part-time pastor than for a full-time pastor.

> While doing this evaluation, I have found the responsibilities for the EM pastor working part-time was very similar for a pastor working full-time.

Christ Centered Preaching

Because preaching is a central part of church life, experienced pastors will spend anywhere between 16–18 hours in sermon preparation. One pastor friend of mine spends 50 hours or more every week preparing for his Sunday message. Although this is irregular, good exegetical preaching does require a lot of prep time. The amount of time for message preparation varies with each individual, but sermon preparation time averages around 30 hours weekly. Good sermons don't come together by Saturday evening. Consistently-solid, theologically-sound sermons don't come easily, even to the most experienced pastors. Some pastors with a speaking gift may be able to prepare a sermon on the morning of the Sunday worship service, but even he won't be able to do it consistently.

When I (Jae) prepare for a message, I have to be thinking about it for weeks. I don't like to speak weekly because of my approach. It's really hard work for me to speak every week because of my desire to "chew" on a subject. Those who are mature in Christ and in tune with the Holy Spirit can usually tell how much time, thought, study, and prayer went into preparing for my sermon.

"Preaching / leading Sunday worship" ranked as the top two priorities. Many of the hiring churches for part-time and full-time pastors desired Christ-centered, inspiring, biblical preaching during their Sunday worship services. Consider this. Whether the preaching is prepared on a part-time or full-time salary, the preparation time is the same which is a serious disadvantage for the part-time pastor who only has about 4 hours left in the week to do everything else after 16 hours of sermon preparation.

Bible Studies and Small Group

Leading Bible studies and small groups ranked the second highest in the list of duties for the part-time pastor. Both Bible studies and sermons require prep time, but if a lay leader is leading the Bible study, the pastor can focus on the sermon and train the layman to lead the Bible study. Unless there is a capable lay leader for the Bible study, when the part-time pastor begins his ministry in a small church, he usually has to do both. This is taxiing on the pastor since the prep times are precluding his shepherding opportunities with the members. Even if the pastor takes the lead in the Bible study, when the congregation grows, he still has to recruit and train leaders to lead the Bible studies and other works of the ministry. This is then the third most desired responsibility for the part-time EM or youth pastor: "Recruit, train, and develop leaders."

Chapter 11

Recruit, Train, and Develop Leaders

How do you recruit and develop leaders?

Even a part-time pastor must recruit, train, and develop lay leaders for the work of the ministry, but it's a time-consuming task.

Ephesians 4:11-12 (NASB)
And He gave some as apostles, and some as prophets, and some as evangelists, and some as pastors and teachers,
for the equipping of the saints for the work of service, to the building up of the body of Christ;

The Bible is clear that pastors are to *"equip the saints for the work of service and build up the body of Christ,"* but this is just one piece of the puzzle. Who is supporting this effort so that the minister can do his job? Jesus didn't have only one disciple helping Him minister to the people; he had a team. For a team to be fully effective at what it does, it takes a minimum of two years, and that's if the pastor is working full-time. Anyone can jump into a pick-up game of basketball, but if you are playing to win, you have to have the right coach with the right players. Training and developing lay leaders to take on the ministry requires experience and expertise. If you are the right leader, then you need the right players on your team.

Even the disciples under Jesus were not fully able to become effective leaders after three years of training. So, asking part-time pastors to recruit, train, and develop leaders in a short period is asking for more than what full time pastors can handle. In the majority of these cases the pastors leave once their seminary education is completed, leaving the church to seek another pastor.

> Playing the game is easy, anyone can play, but winning a game means that you have to have the right coach with the right players.

Just because a couple has a newborn baby does not make them expert parents. Good parenting requires knowledge, experience, discernment, and determination. And just because a pastor has a PhD or a Master of Divinity does not automatically make him proficient in recruiting, training, and developing leaders unless that was his field of study, and he has experience doing it. Not all pastors have the gift, experience, or skill set to be this kind of leader. When the Hiring Church presumably expects any pastor to have these leadership skills, they are in for some disappointment.

Most seminaries do not have classes that teach students how to recruit, train, and develop a team. This is typically taught in a business school or an MBA program. Some seminaries will have courses on spiritual leadership, but there is no real and practical way of applying the specific skill set of recruiting, developing, and training leaders in a classroom.

The majority of the leaders with this particular style of gift and or learned skill set have a background in one or more of the following categories:

1. Coaching (participated as a sports coach for more than three years).

2. Professional career in management / supervisor / director / human resource / executive.

3. Small business owner with more than five years of experience with employees that are non-family members and whose turn-over rate was low.

4. Ministers who have planted a church and have experience in hiring and training leaders for ministry.

5. Executive and or associate pastor who have extensive leadership training in recruitment and training leaders to replace themselves and have hired and fired staff.

6. A ministry leader who has been involved extensively in discipleship.

7. People in business or ministry fields that have experience in recruiting, training, and developing leaders or volunteers to fulfill set tasks or goals.

Leaders with the background mentioned above are apt to vision-cast, motivate, and encourage people toward a noble purpose. Even though the full-time pastor might be lacking in one or more of the skill set to recruit, train, and develop leaders, he will have time, if he is supported by the Head Church, to develop these skills to accomplish the church ministry goals. When lacking in this leadership skill set, the full-time pastor must be given time and energy to focus and develop these specific skills.

Some leaders will have the skills necessary to train leaders within a two year period, but if the skills are not there, the pastor will need at least three years to build lay leaders. The full-time pastor with a long-term vision for the church can eventually recruit, train, and develop leaders for ministry objectives but only with the long term support from the Head Church.

A former college pastor who was interviewed for this book talked about his frustration with his EM pastor's leadership. The EM pastor did not have the background or the understanding of how to coach the people underneath him, so when concerns were brought up by the college pastor, the EM pastor's ability to guide and coach his leaders fell short. And this is the reason EM pastors fail when planting an independent EM church.

So, What Can the Hiring Church Do?

1. First, find out if this is really necessary based on the identity, core values, and overarching goal of the Head Church. Many churches will conclude that recruiting and developing leaders is really not suitable for part-time pastors to handle. Focusing on the spiritual growth of the members and shepherding them are more appropriate for part-time ministers.

2. Find out from the EM pastor if he actually has the spiritual gift of leadership (Leadership should be ranked either

number 1 or 2 on the spiritual gift evaluation) and if it has been tested by his life experience. The hiring church must then reduce their expectations on shepherding, counseling, and nurturing when hiring a minister with leadership gifts. Rarely, will one pastor be skilled in both leadership and nurture.

3. If the EM pastor does not have leadership skills the church is looking for, then finding a lay leader to support the part-time EM pastor is the next best thing. Team ministry is the best way to have an effective and successful ministry.

4. If the EM pastor or any of the lay leaders of the church does not have the spiritual gift of leadership, then find a passionate leader who desires to lead. During the interview process the candidate should be informed that he is not expected to nurture and counsel his flock to the degree that he is expected to lead them. This emphasis should be noted on the responsibilities section of the job description.

Prioritizing Responsibilities for the Part-time Pastor

Many churches do not prioritize the list of responsibilities before hiring an EM pastor. After preaching they are undecided as to which one should be next in importance.

1. Preaching / leading Sunday worship
2. Leading Bible studies / small groups
3. Training and developing leaders

4. Working with pastoral staff

5. Pastoral care / counseling

6. Spiritual leadership and direction

7. Planning / coordination / activities and events

8. Motivating congregation to serve

9. Willing to support vision

Sample Questions:

1. Should we give priority to training and developing leaders or to developing small groups?

2. Should counseling someone be more important than developing and training leaders?

3. Should establishing relationships and nurturing the youth and college students be more important than planning and running events?

4. How long do we desire the EM/youth pastor to stay?

5. At what length of term and estimated time do we hope to financially support the part-time pastor to become full-time with benefits and at what salary?

The Hiring Church should first understand their priorities by asking the questions mentioned above. Prioritizing will clarify the reasons for hiring a part-time EM/youth pastor and the duration he is needed for the task. In addition, the Hiring Church should have some basic idea of the time frame for promoting the part-time pastor to full-time with salary and benefits. This will create in the candidate a long-term mindset. Something that is good for both parties. If it is not explained and understood from the beginning, the part-time pastor will plan on exiting the church once the commitment period has been met. If it is known that the part-time pastor will be graduating from seminary in 2 years but the Hiring Church is uncertain that the membership will be big enough to support a full-time EM position by then, it will be prudent to set 2-year goals. This will give the part-time pastors a time frame to complete the task he has been hired to do in preparation for the next part-time EM/youth pastor.

Because the part-time pastor is in a time sensitive situation with other important jobs in his life such as seminary, work, and family life, the Head Church must set the priorities for him. Without them the church will be disappointed because only a little in each category will be accomplished, and the pastor will feel the weight of the task that now burdens him because he too sees the lack of progress.

First Set of Directions:

1. The hiring committee and the core members of the EM congregation should set up a meeting to go over the list first. (It is recommended that each member of the hiring committee have his own book, "Hiring an English Ministry Pastor & Beyond" to fill out the questions)

2. Brainstorm and pray about the area that needs to be filled in if it is not already written.

3. Make sure that the Senior Pastor is involved in filling out this section. (The Senior Pastor should understand the needs and desires of the EM congregation.)

4. Rank the responsibilities in the order of importance, the highest rank being 1.

Prioritizing the Responsibilities

Category	Rank
Other: _____	_____
Leading Bible studies	_____
Developing small groups	_____
Pastoral care (hospital visits, shepherding, etc.)	_____
Spiritual leadership (prayer, management, etc.)	_____
Vision casting	_____
Preaching / leading Sunday worship	_____
Motivating congregation to serve	_____
Planning and coordinating activities and events	_____
Counseling	_____
Working with staff (Korean/Chinese context)	_____
Committed to leadership of EM/Youth (What is the desired length of time?)	
Other: _____	_____
Other: _____	_____

Second Set of Directions:

1. On a board write down the list from the most important to the least important.

2. The goal is to reduce list of responsibilities to the five most important ones.

3. Now, reduce the list to three most important responsibilities for the EM/youth pastor to accomplish. Now approximate the time required to fulfill those responsibilities, including preparation, travel, and implementation. If there is still time left over, priorities 4 and 5 can be considered.

Note: Prioritizing the responsibilities along with a time frame in which to accomplish them will clarify for the new pastor what he is expected to do. Without the objectives the pastor will come up with his own goals for the church.

Top Five Areas of Ministry Desired by the Church

1. _____

_____

2. _____

_____

3. _____

_____

4. _____

_____

5. _____

_____

Part-time pastors who are committed to a certain time frame (1-2 years), should be limited to three primary responsibilities with the option of completing the remaining two if time permits.

The Basics of Recruiting

EM pastor or not, make a strong commitment to recruit. You will need it. Recruiting people for any volunteer work or leadership position is neither simple nor easy, but it is rewarding, and it's the backbone of ministry. Lay leadership is not built over night so be patient, but intentional.

If you feel that you are not able to make this commitment, then finding someone who can, will be vital to the recruitment process. Furthermore, if you are not the primary decision maker, then it is important to receive full support from your supervisor. The recruitment process is a long term objective and not a short term solution, and it never ends. Just like a company that hires and retires employees, you will be recruiting and retiring volunteer leaders. Here's how to begin:

1. A good way to recruit potential leaders is simply to make the announcement that you are recruiting those who have interest in leadership. Before you do, have a plan of action

124

for training and discipling these potential leaders. During the recruitment process, try not to look for experience as a requirement for leadership. As long as member is teachable, he can learn and mature into the role. When you do advertise your need, have volunteers give testimonies either in the pulpit, during fellowship and or small groups. The announcements should be short and encouraging.

2. Hold a spiritual gifts assessment class to find out what skill set your congregation members have. Have repeat classes so that everyone has the opportunity to attend. Make the net as large as possible so you can catch the most number of fish. (One church used media-savvy volunteers to let the people know of their recruitment goals. It was very successful.)

3. A personal invitation is the most effective way to recruit. Special attention from the pastor is a compliment and everyone knows it. Even if they don't participate now, it will sow seeds for any other position that they may be a match for. Meeting at the office is good, but having a meal together to discuss the subject is even better. Tell him exactly what you're looking for and why you think he will be a great addition to the team.

4. Instead of doing the recruitment yourself, let leaders in your team take the helm as part of their training process. All leaders need to recruit. For example, a small group leader recruits a volunteer to show how it's done. He trains the rookie for a year and begins the process with someone else. In this way there is on-going recruitment with every small

group leader. This particular reproduction approach has been used successfully in many large churches, but can also be applied effectively in small churches. The key to this approach is the foundation. You must train the first set of leaders properly. Because they will be doing the subsequent training, invest more time in them. You will reap great dividends if you do. It's like raising kids. If you train the first child right, the siblings will have a good example to follow. If the first child isn't trained properly, the siblings will learn his bad habits. And handing a leader a book and wishing him the best is not good leadership training. Personalized instruction with encouragement is the pathway to success in training a volunteer.

Ask for help from other churches. For small churches with limited resources, partnering with other small or large churches to recruit and train volunteers lightens the load for both churches. (American churches have been known to support smaller ethnic churches with resources and training.)

From the Heart of an EM Pastor

Part of my job was to recruit and train volunteers for a new ministry. I asked the leadership to give me three months to evaluate the congregation first, before implementing this new ministry. I first needed to see if it was even feasible to implement this new ministry, if we had no people running it. The ministry sounded very exciting and was also in need, but it was also vital to see if there would even be participation in it. Without any participants and volunteers, the ministry would fall in just months. I spoke with people first to see if there might be some interest and if so, if they would be willing to participate if it happened. I asked if I could take their name, number, and emails to connect with them, when this new ministry took off. The people's commitment and willingness to participate was a sure sign of success before the new ministry began. A core team of seven was established and a two month prayer and training session was pre-launched with a set date to fully launch with other members. The key was for me to find a committed team which created success for this ministry. We made the announcement directly from the pulpit, but I found out that approaching the people directly made the difference between people who were thinking about it and were excited about it. What I realized was that when I was excited about the new ministry, the people got excited about it as well.

Chapter 12

Priorities in Life

What are your priorities?

The priorities of the EM/youth pastor drive what he does in ministry. The high expectations placed upon a part-time pastor are guaranteed to send him packing unless his priorities are understood and supported. The Hiring Church can demonstrate a team spirit by working with the pastor toward a schedule that is mutually agreeable. This will encourage the pastor to serve with focus and motivation. The pastor cannot feel used and abused only to be discarded before the next pastor arrives. In order to establish a win-win situation, both parties must work toward agreed-upon goals. This will create a healthy environment for the members of the church to thrive. Below is a general list of priorities for many part-time EM/youth pastors:

1. God: Spending quiet time in prayer and the Word. Understanding his calling and purpose.

2. Wife: Meeting her emotional needs of protection and provision

3. Children: Instructing them in the word and showing them affection

4. Finance / money (financial security to support family tuition for school)

5. Seminary (if still attending school: studying to finish the degree)

6. Work (other part-time jobs to supplement income)

7. Friends (being able to release stress in life; accountability)

8. Worship (being able to attend service for spiritual growth)

9. Church job and ministry experience

Pastors will have similar category of priorities but not necessarily in the same order. Everything that concerns EM/Youth pastors will generally fit into the listed areas. Below is the list for myself when I was a part-time EM pastor.

1. God: Spending quiet time in prayer and the Word.

2. Myself: Constantly striving to become a better husband, father and leader.

3. Wife: Meeting her emotional needs of protection and provision

4. Children: Instructing them in the word and showing them affection

5. Learning from mentors and spiritual friends

6. Church (being able to attend service for spiritual growth)

7. Projects / church work

:rmons, Bible study, etc)

ıp late to his staff meeting because his wife
During the meeting his wife kept calling so the KM Pastor asked who it was. The EM Pastor explained that his wife was sick and was trying to reach him to tell him to get some medicine from the pharmacy. The KM Pastor got upset that she kept calling him in the middle of an important meeting. The pastor blurted out, "We all have to make sacrifice to serve Christ. Turn off the phone!"

The KM Pastor pierced the heart of the EM Pastor. The EM Pastor's wife was very high on his priority list and the job at the church was at the very bottom. If the ministry philosophy of the KM Pastor keeps clashing with the EM Pastor's priorities, the EM Pastor will seek another ministry to serve, one that will be more accommodating of his needs.

> The EM pastor's wife was very high on his priority list and the job at the church was at the very bottom.

It is cultural to expect the younger to serve the older, but like a son that gets fed up with his parents and leaves his home at the age of 18, the EM Pastor will not be motivated to serve in a Korean church if he feels that the church is only taking and not giving. The Hiring Church must consider how to invest in the pastor for the advancement of his character and the good of the kingdom.

Matthew 28:19

Go therefore and make disciples of all nations, baptizing them in the name of the Father and of the Son and of the Holy Spirit.

Disciple making is a mandate for every Christian and for every church for all time. Training others to be like Christ should pepper everything that we do from the Sr. Pastor to the new believer. Jesus instructed all His followers to take part in discipling the lost, and He modeled this lifestyle for us during His earthly ministry. The New Testament disciples obeyed His command, and their efforts are recorded in the book of Acts and the epistles. The pastor will have the most lasting impact by building into the leadership of his church rather than focusing on the congregation. This includes the EM Pastor who is under his care.

When I worked at a large multicultural church, I attended an important directors' meeting, where all the pastors and directors came together to go over a very important event. During the meeting my wife kept calling on the phone. Even though it was on vibrate, everyone could hear it. The executive pastor soon asked, "Well! Aren't you going to answer that call?" I responded, "No, it's just my wife. I can call her after the meeting." This response did not fare well with the leadership team. The executive pastor urged, "If it's your wife, you'd better answer that phone! Here at our church, we place our family first before our ministry." (If you are a first gen Asian, you may thinking that what just happened was immature, and they don't have their priority straight, but the second gen Asian is thinking the very opposite. Who's right?)

On another occasion I came in late to work, and very casually, my supervisor asked how my family was doing. I let him know that

I was late because my wife was sick, and I was trying to help her with the children. He looked bewildered and questioned, "Why are you here? You should be home taking care of your wife and children. Go home. God will take care of His ministry. He can do it without you."

Well, number two on my priority list is "Myself" for becoming a better husband and father. Because the ministry philosophy with the church matched my priorities, I took off without worrying about what the leadership would think of me, the new pastor.

> Because the ministry philosophy with the church matched my priorities, I took off without worrying about what the leadership would think of me, the new pastor.

I started working for this American church part-time because the values of the church matched my priorities. In less than six months the church offered a full-time position and I gladly accepted.

The EM pastor, whether he is working part-time or full-time knows he must have a good relationship with his church leadership, and not meeting each other's needs will always create conflict. Dr. Willard Harley, one of the most respected marriage counselors in the world, writes in his book *His Needs Her Needs*, "*Marital conflict is created one of two ways: (1) Couples fail to make each other happy, or (2) couples make each other unhappy. In the first case couples are frustrated because their needs are not being met. In the second case they're deliberately hurting each other. I call the first cause of conflict failure to care and the second, failure to protect."* [12]

What Dr. Harley says applies to the relationship between the EM pastor and the KM leadership. When both parties fail to make each other happy or support each other's priorities or when both parties make each other unhappy, frustration occurs. And when frustrations are not dealt with, separation will result.

To the EM Pastor, "List your priorities."

1. _____

2. _____

3. _____

4. _____

5. _____

6. _____

7. _____

8. _____

9. _____

10. _____

11. _____

12. _____

13. _____

14. _____

Chapter 13

Focus, Energy, and Time for Ministry Effectiveness

Do you have enough energy to build a successful ministry?

How much focus, energy, and time are required for the pastor to do his job effectively. The questions to consider are as follows:

1. What are the most important things **in** my life?

2. What are the most important things **for** my life?

3. What occupies or will occupy my thoughts most?

4. What determines or will determine the most energy exertion? The giving of energy to complete the task.

5. What takes up most of my time because it is necessity or required?

When coming up with possible answers to each question, brainstorm for at least three answers per question. Pray through the list, and see if it lines up with Lord's direction for that ministry.

A Korean church asked if I could help them on a pa
even though I was already working full-time for anothei
set a very specific time commitment and some boundaries w
Korean church, and let them know clearly my priorities for t.
ministry. I didn't want to just create a little excitement in thei.
ministry and disappear without leaving lasting impact. A time
commitment was set for one year for the training of cell group
leaders so they would be able to lead on their own after the training
period. I asked a very specific question to God, "What is my
purpose for this church?" The convictions were clear: build
relationships with the cell group leaders and establish their
foundation with Christ as future leaders. The Lord showed what I
needed to focus on, and I knew how much energy and time I could
put into the calling. I went into the agreement clear-headed. And
when all was said and done, I knew I had completed the work He
gave me to do.

How do you maintain balance so you don't get burnt out?

Congregation members or people in general either drain you or
energize you. Nobody goes through ministry without running into
certain people who suck out his energy like a vacuum so that by the
time he gets home he needs a nap! Then there are some people who
give us so much energy that even when we get home, we're still
thinking about what was said or done. Before you get hired or
shortly afterwards, find someone who will fill you with energy

perience or insight. Those individuals are
ne. It might even be the Sr. Pastor.

? has a Christian mentor to help him
successful businessman as mentor for
ɔns. He speaks with an out-of-state friend once a
about life and for prayer, and he has a hang-out buddy for
leisure activities. There are four areas of his needs being addressed
with close relationships. He has good support outside of ministry
which will help him last in ministry.

During my ministry at an American church, I had an elder as a
mentor. He was a man of integrity and constant prayer so I trusted
his counsel concerning my personal life. For ministry questions I
had another mentor who spoke with great words of wisdom. He
helped me to understand how to minister to the church members. I
also sought out an experienced Christian counselor who became a
friend and mentor because we worked together to minister to the
hurting and distressed. There were also two friends who were my
accountability partners. Every Monday morning for a year we sent
weekly summary reports of what God was doing in our personal
lives, which included both praise and prayer requests. Once a
month we had a conference call lifting one another up in prayer and
just enjoying each other's company. These were people that gave
me energy, so I could tackle the "spiritual battles" we all face every
day.

Many parents of EM pastors ran businesses or just worked long
hours and sacrificed time for their children. In order to prevent their
children from feeling what they felt because their parents were
away so much, 2nd gen pastors covet their time with their children.
They want to give as much time to their children as a reasonable

schedule will allow. This is why their balancing act is so difficult. They want to be effective in ministry, but they don't want to sacrifice their children to achieve it.

Much like the parents of 2nd gen pastors, 1st gen pastors give so much of their energy, time, and focus to the church that their children feel neglected. I (Jae) had a pastor's son come into my office and while we were talking, with tears in his eyes he shared that he hardly saw his dad. Now, as a married man with a son himself he doesn't treat church as a priority. He seems to be going through the motions, and I wonder if it's because he thinks church took his dad away and so he bears a grudge against it. But the 1st gen pastor is fully convinced that serving the church means less time with his wife and children. Both he and his 1st gen congregation believe that it is noble and more importantly, pleasing to God. They can't understand why EM pastors need to go to their kids' soccer games when they should be doing something important like training leaders for the next mission trip. There is a big difference between the priorities of the EM pastors and the 1st gen pastors.

This is the reason every EM pastor should find a mentor. The mentor can help him balance his life, both in ministry and personal life. This mentor can be a sounding board and accountability partner so when the pastor sets his priorities and deviates from them, the mentor can step in and put him back on course. The ideal situation is to have a mentor before going into ministry, especially one who is a veteran in the field. If not, finding one soon after entering the ministry will serve the pastor well. If the pastor doesn't find a mentor within the first two years, ministry life could do irreparable damage to his longevity. And because pastors begin deciding whether to leave or stay within the first 2 years of their service, making sure that the ministry experience is positive must be a priority. Additionally, after two years it is more difficult for young pastors to find mentors, not because they don't want them but because the pastors are too engrossed in ministry to look.

I spoke with an EM pastor in California who had a large, rapidly-growing, EM congregation. He was looking to add another associate pastor who would run the church's many programs. He wanted the pastor to run as fast as he could when they hired him. I didn't say anything, but when you speed through ministry, not only will you tire out your congregation and leave them behind, but you will have sprinted past the Lord, running over the one who should be leading. The diagram below is a picture of a balanced perspective for an EM pastor:

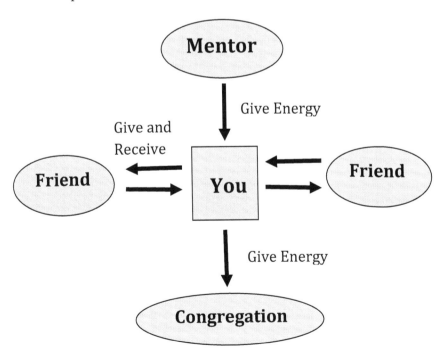

Finding a Mentor

It may difficult for an EM pastor to find a good mentor within the church. The primary issue is "transparency." The Asian culture avoids the appearance of weakness by hiding it in so it is difficult to share what sounds like a weakness with a member of the church, especially a leader. Problems in the family bring "shame" which must be avoided at almost all costs. It isn't until it gets totally unbearable that an Asian would seek help. Rather than talk about their issues, Asians do the "spiritual" thing. They pray. This is one of the reasons why many 1st immigrant Korean churches have "early morning prayer" services. The pain and sorrow must be expressed, but they can't tell anyone and because they know God won't tell anyone, they tell Him.

Christian counselors in Korean churches would have a very difficult time finding clients. In fact a seminary degree related to pastoral counseling in South Korea is very scarce. Foreign believers who go to South Korea see a nation that prays, but in reality the Christians are praying because they want counseling—from God and no one else.

How do you find a mentor in an Asian-American church?

When I was an EM pastor, I knew the importance of establishing a personal relationship with other leaders. Connection, trust, and loyalty were the principles I strived for with the 1st gen Korean pastor. It is not typical for a younger EM pastor to invite the senior pastor to his house for dinner. But I did that for three primary reasons.

1. ***Respect:*** As the new EM pastor on staff, I wanted to show my respect to the elder pastor.

2. ***Relationship-building through food:*** Food is central in establishing an open relationship in many Asian cultures and eating together draws people close because it recreates a family setting. The main dishes are placed in the center of the table so everyone including guests can feel like part of the family. This is the reason why I invited the KM pastor and his family for dinner. I wanted him to know that I consider him as family and I was open to learning from him and willing to seek his advice and counsel. Even if you are not able to speak Korean or Chinese fluently, the 1st immigrant pastor will greatly appreciate your effort to communicate with him and the love you're showing in feeding him a well-cooked meal. Ultimately, it is your heart that will win him over, so make the effort, enjoy the closeness and food.

3. ***Introduction to my wife and family:*** Many Korean churches expect the pastor's wife to serve in some capacity, and when the wife does not serve, the church is disappointed. My goal was to share with the senior pastor and his wife the passion my wife had for ministry. This was more of a defensive mechanism. I wanted the pastor to be aware of her desires in case she was falsely accused of not being my ministry partner.

During my tenure at the church, I learned so much from my elder leader and his life journeys. Because of this early establishment of openness, I found out that he used to be a collegiate gymnast, and at his old age he was still able to walk on his hands. He actually demonstrated his ability in front of my family. The fact that he became a pastor was truly a testament to his mother's fervent "early morning prayers." She prayed and fasted during his fight against God's calling to enter the ministry. My relationship with my elder KM pastor is still great. He was a great mentor to me. A good mentor relationship will increase long-term ministry effectiveness.

Difficulty in Finding a Mentor?

There is a multi-cultural group of EM pastors of Korean, Chinese, American, and Jamaican (Huh? Yes, Jamaican) descent that gather once a month in Maryland. They gather together to encourage one another in their "labor" so that no one feels alone during the trials and tribulations of ministry. It is sometimes a support group, a think tank, a network, a sounding board, and a sibling group, but mostly it's a refuge. They are ministers who love one another, and anyone who goes there will feel it no matter how new he may be. Burdens brought there are lifted, joys shared there are multiplied, and no one leaves without being encouraged. They have been a great group of pastors for many years. EM pastors should have a mentor and a support group to help them last in ministry.

Chapter 14

Moses Had a Great Mentor

Who is your mentor?

The Bible has many examples of mentoring relationships; Barnabas and Saul, Paul and Timothy, and Jesus and the disciples to just mention a few. The one that strikes me the most was the mentor of one of the most powerful and influential Hebrew leaders. His name was Jethro, the priest of Midian and father-in-law of Moses, and who *"heard of everything God had done for Moses and for his people Israel, and how the Lord had brought Israel out of Egypt"* (Ex. 18:1). Moses had shown great leadership in guiding his people from the hands of the mighty Pharaoh. Yet, it was Jethro who helped the celebrated leader of the Israelites become the great judge.

What are the characteristics of a good mentor?

As good mentors do, Jethro must have built a good relationship with Moses in order to receive such respect in front of everyone, *"So Moses went out to meet his father-in-law and bowed down and kissed him"(v 7)*. Moses' action indicates a good, healthy, and productive relationship with his father-in-law. The relationship was close enough for Moses to confide in him. . . *"about everything the LORD had done to Pharaoh and the Egyptians for Israel's sake and about all the hardships they had met along the way and how the LORD had saved them"(18:8).*

Jethro sat through and listened to *"everything God had done"* and was *"delighted to hear about all the good things" (v 9).* Jethro had great listening skills and visibly showed his joy of hearing about God's work in the Israelites. He was attentive and gave positive reinforcement. Moses' father-in-law sets the example by leading Moses to offer sacrifices to God. How could this be? It was Moses who led the people out of Egypt, and yet it was Jethro who reminded Moses to always go back to God. Jethro did this by first offering praise for the deliverance of Israel and then leading him to offer sacrifices to the Lord. A mentor will always lead the heart of his students back to God. He knows where the glory belongs:

Exodus 18:10-12

[10] He said, "Praise be to the LORD, who rescued you from the hand of the Egyptians and of Pharaoh, and who rescued the people from the hand of the Egyptians. [11] Now I know that the LORD is greater than all other gods, for he did this to those who had treated Israel arrogantly." [12] Then Jethro, Moses' father-in-law, brought a burnt offering and other sacrifices to God, and Aaron came with all the elders of Israel to eat bread with Moses' father-in-law in the presence of God.

A good mentor is also a patient observer (vv 13-14). His father-in-law watched from morning till evening all that Moses was doing for the people as their judge. Sitting through and paying close attention to Moses explaining God's decrees and laws is a laborious task which takes great patience.

Jethro as a mentor to Moses shows concern for his well-being. *"What you are doing is not good. You and these people who come to you will only wear yourselves out. The work is too heavy for you; you cannot handle it alone" (vv 17-18).* Moses' father-in-law knew what Moses was doing was detrimental to his health and would not be able to lead his people if this burdensome work continued. Moses didn't even realize the amount of pressure and unnecessary burden he was putting on himself, and it took a discerning pair of eyes to see what Moses himself could not see. Moses knew this, but he needed to have confirmation from an admired and trusted leader. His heart was now open to hearing his mentor. After hearing his father-in-law's advice, Moses was rejuvenated, and shortly afterward he took action.

Exodus 18:24-27

[24] *Moses listened to his father-in-law and did everything he said.* [25] *He chose capable men from all Israel and made them leaders of the people, officials over thousands, hundreds, fifties and tens.* [26] *They served as judges for the people at all times. The difficult cases they brought to Moses, but the simple ones they decided themselves.*
[27] *Then Moses sent his father-in-law on his way, and Jethro returned to his own country.*

One of the most important aspects of finding a mentor is that the person seeking a mentor must have a teachable heart. You can find the best formal and informal mentors, but if the person seeking a mentor does not have a humble heart that is willing to listen and learn, then he won't improve. Moses humbled himself to learn from his father-in-law because he had a teachable heart. This is when he went from a good leader to an exemplary one. God will bring people into our lives to give us a sense of balance, to handle the difficult challenges that we often face. Moses learned from Jethro's wisdom how to manage his focus, energy, and time.

Who is your mentor?

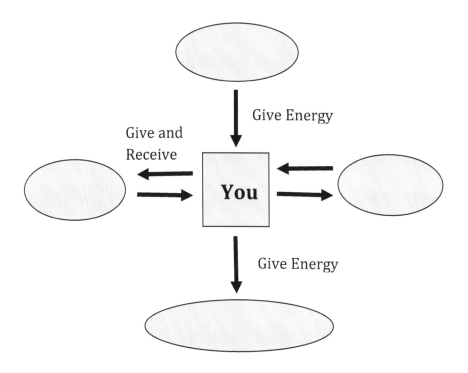

Do you have any mentors? If "Yes" please write their names:

1. _____

2. _____

3. _____

Are you a mentor to someone? Yes _____ No _____

Are you involved with any accountability group?

Yes _____

No _____

In the process of getting involved in one _____

In the process of developing one _____

Other:

_____

_____

_____

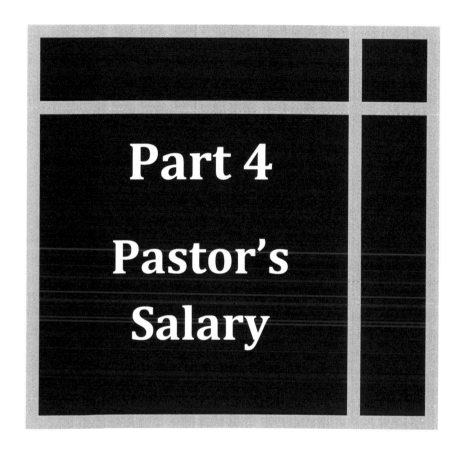

Part 4

Pastor's
Salary

Four nearly two decades, John R. Cionca has studied numerous cases of pastoral transitions and he noted, *"Although restlessness is sometimes sovereignly aroused, more typically this feeling of unsettledness is situationally related. Personal time-tables and expectations, ministerial pressures, criticisms, family harmony, financial concerns, and life-cycle factors affect a pastor's sense of accomplishment."*[13] In many Asian churches the financial concerns of the pastors are typically not openly discussed. Contrary to that many American churches have annual salary reviews. Performance or salary reviews are virtually unheard of in Asian American churches. In most cases whatever salary the pastor is offered at the time of hiring is normally what the pastor will continue to get even when additional family members are added to his household.

4

Pastor's Salary

> *Personal time-tables and expectations, ministerial pressures, criticisms, family harmony, financial concerns, and life-cycle factors affect a pastor's sense of accomplishment. –*
>
> John R. Cionca

Chapter 15

Pastor's Salary

How much should we pay the pastor?

Pastor Bob went to California to be interviewed as the new EM pastor of a good size EM congregation. The youth ministry was already established, and the EM was 40% singles, 40% college students, and 20% young married couples. Northern California has a growing pan-Asian community, and the church was near a university so it attracted many visitors.

Pastor Bob did an extensive research on the church and the surrounding areas. The potential of this church excited him. He felt at peace with this congregation.. Almost everything about his passion seemed to fit the identity of the EM congregation. But there was one major hesitation. For the full-time position he was offered $3,000 per month, with housing allowance, full healthcare, and other ministry benefits. He knew that he would be taking a cut from his former IT job where he earned about $75,000 per year. But he didn't realize that this was the average salary that EM pastors were getting across the country. According to the U.S. Census Bureau, Pastor Bob was being offered a salary equivalent to that of a high school graduate. Unsurprisingly, the pastor and his wife decided that this was not the right church for them.

Thankfully for the church, they were able to hire an unmarried, seminary student, willing to take the low pay, but unfortunately for church, once he finishes school and gets married, he too will leave for a job that pays sufficiently to sustain his family and give him financial stability. Ultimately, the Korean church will continue on a vicious cycle, trying to keep an EM pastor on staff until it decides to amply provide the minister for his services.

According to the U.S. Census Bureau, Pastor Bob was being offered a salary equivalent to that of a high school graduate.

The 2007 Official USDA Food Plan [14] calculates the average monthly food expense for children between 1 – 11 years of age:

Monthly low cost plan per child	$131.42
Moderate cost plan per child	$160.48
Liberal cost plan per child	$191.50

Using the USDA Food Plan and the general calculation of all the expenses for his family, Pastor Bob needed a minimum of $4,500 to live in that area. Because God had given his wife the calling to be a missionary to their children, she was a stay-at-home mom. She was fulfilling her role as a wife, and that left Pastor Bob the full burden of providing for the family.

Average Salary for EM Pastors

As of March 2011 the average pay for an EM pastor working part-time was $1,500/month and full-time was $3,000/month. Over the years the cost of living expenses have gone up but the salaries have not. Family is a priority for EM pastors and making sure that their children are well fed is not only their concern but also the hiring church's, if it wants to attract capable pastors.

Paying the EM pastors a low salary has not changed for over a decade in many Korean churches. While gas and other prices have increased since the mid 1990s, the traditional pay structure for an EM pastor crawled compared to the speed of living expenses. Even the minimum low wage has doubled since the 90s, but Korean churches have been very slow to catch up to the current pay structure. The yearly salary review is unheard of in small to medium size churches. So, when the EM pastor gets married and plans to have children, the couple will consider salary rates of churches before they decide where to serve. EM pastors will put their family's needs first so Korean churches that match their financial needs will have a greater chance of keeping them on a long-term basis.

Korean churches usually don't post how much they're willing to pay the EM pastor or even mention the range of salary. The choice of words for salary are usually "negotiable based on qualification and experience" or "competitive salary" but only a few are bold enough to post a pay offer to attract an EM pastor. The 1st gen ministry philosophy of "sacrifice for the church" makes most Asian churches reluctant to reserve competitive salary rates for EM pastors.

The hiring churches that are aggressive in their recruitment process specify their salary. Below are some samples:

State	Position	Type	Salary
New Jersey	EM pastor	Part-time	$2,000 / month
New Jersey	EM pastor	Part-time	$2,500 / month
Virginia	EM pastor	Full-time	$50,000 / year
Tennessee	EM pastor	Full-time	$35 - $50,000 / year
California	EM pastor	Full-time	$50 - $60,000 / year

These were negotiable based upon qualifications and experience, but the majority of the churches still offered an average of $1,500 for part-time and $37,500 per year for full-time. The average yearly earnings for an assistant pastor in Korean churches is $25,000 - $30,000 per year and for an associate pastor it's $35,000 - $40,000 per year.

There are three reasons that majority of the KM churches maintained such a low average wage for over a decade.

1. "This is what other Korean churches pay," was the mind set.

2. "This is what we have always paid," was their justification.

3. "This is what the elders proposed," was their excuse.

The traditional perspective is that no staff member should be paid more than the senior pastor, which is reasonable. After all he oversees everything. But even before salary negotiations and without knowing the candidate's family situation, many churches will have already decided the salary amount. Without doing any research and not knowing where to obtain the information to determine a ministry pay structure, many will continue to follow tradition when it comes to compensation.

Chapter 16

The Average Pay Structure for Church Staff

> The average pay for a senior pastor is
> $80,000

The *2009 Compensation Handbook for Church Staff* reported that the average earnings for a senior pastor was $80,000.[15] The survey included close to 5,000 denominational and independent churches across the United States. This comprehensive handbook is a compilation of extensive research on church staff compensation plans. Churches can easily determine the base salary, retirement, health insurance, housing allowance & parsonage, life insurance, and continuing education allowances for potential staff members. In addition, churches can determine the compensation levels for solo pastors, associate pastors, executive/administrative pastors, youth pastors, music directors, and even part-time custodians. Each year there is a new Compensation Handbook that can assist church leaders with their salary reviews.

The compensation packages, including benefits such as retirement, life insurance, health insurance, and continuing education, has increased to $81,113 per year for the average senior pastor according to the *2009 Compensation Handbook*. The handbook further explains that pastors who have higher academic degrees are paid up to $30,000 more per year than pastors without any post-secondary education.

The 2009 Compensation Plan survey reports that churches that draw 101 to 300 people each week pay senior pastors $72,664 per year, including benefits. The pay increases to $88,502 for pastors at churches that average a weekly attendance of 301 to 500 people, and then to $102,623 when attendance averages 501 to 750 people. Compensation also increased to $60,777 for executive and administrative pastors at churches averaging 101 to 300 people and to $76,671 at churches of 501 to 750 in attendance.

According to the handbook, the salary is also different among denominations. Presbyterian and Lutheran churches pay pastors the most with over $100,000. Executive and administrative pastors make more on average with independent and non-denominational churches; the average pay being $80,469. According to the survey, the average compensation in Baptist denominations are:

- Full-Time Senior Pastor $79,855

- Full-Time Solo Pastor $54,456

- Full-Time Administrative Pastor $80,469

- Full-Time Associate Pastor $60,505

- Part-Time Associate Pastor $14,397

- Full-Time Christian Ed Pastor $61,509

- Full-Time Youth Pastor $52,043

- Part-Time Youth Pastor $10,660

- Full-Time Children's Pastor $50,887

- Full-Time Worship Pastor $66,588

- Full-Time Church Secretary $29,381

- Part-Time Church Secretary $12,059

- Full-Time Church Custodian $36,094

- Part-Time Church Custodian $7,108

This report is from the *2009 Compensation Handbook for Church Staff*. The full report shows how church salaries vary according to the size of the church income, church attendance, geographical region, education, and years employed.

Are the churches using handbooks like these to compensate God's gifted and talented servants adequately? Are these salaries reasonable and fair? Or are we letting the world take some of the brightest and most gifted servants from the churches by offering less than they deserve?

During the recession of 2008–2009 the average salary was the following:

o High School graduate $23,400 - $30,400

o Associate's degree $36,800 - $38,200

o Bachelor's degree $52,200

o Master's degree $62,300

o Doctoral degree $89,400

The 2008–2009 average salary earned is similar to the standard earned salary recommended by the U.S. Census Bureau in 2003.

Source: U.S. Census Bureau based on median income by highest degree earned for male[16]

2003 U.S. Census Bureau - average salary for male age 25+

- High School graduate $28,763
- Associate's degree $39,015
- Bachelor's degree $50,916
- Master's degree $61,698
- Doctorate degree $73,853

2007 U.S. Census Bureau – average salary male with the following degrees

- High School graduate $36,839
- Associate's degree $47,190
- Bachelor's degree $70,898
- Master's degree $86,966
- Doctorate degree $108,941

Salaries from 2003 - 2009

- High School graduate $25,000 - $35,000
- Associate's degree $35,000 - $50,000
- Bachelor's degree $50,000 - $65,000
- Master's degree $60,000 - $75,000
- Doctoral degree $80,000 - $95,000
- Pastors with Master of Divinity degree

  $70,000 - $80,000
- EM pastors with Master of Divinity degree

  $35,000 - $45,000

Size of Congregation Compared to Pastor's Salary

Congregation Size	Senior Pastor's Salary
101 – 300	$72,664 plus benefits
301 – 500	$88,502 plus benefits
501 – 750	$102,623 plus benefits

Jim Rickard is a certified public accountant and the director of Stewardship Services Foundation, which advises churches and pastors about financial issues. His foundation prepares tax returns for more than 2,000 pastors across United States. Rickard explains, *"A pastor requires a cash salary to meet his family's physical needs independent of his wife having to work. A good starting point would be to review their personal budget and build on it. A pastor who struggles to provide for his family will hesitate to teach biblical stewardship from the pulpit. If he can't live it, he shouldn't teach it."*[17]

> *A pastor who struggles to provide for his family will hesitate to teach biblical stewardship from the pulpit. If he can't live it, he shouldn't teach it.* – Jim Rickard

Now we can understand better why Pastor Bob decided to work for another Korean church, one that was willing to match his priorities for his family's security. Any church that was willing to follow God's directive for adequately providing for its minister is a church worth serving. Pastor Bob was now able to focus on ministry development because his attention is no longer diverted by his financial situation.

Why should the pastor be given an adequate salary?

The church should be offering a competitive salary, especially if the pastor has achieved a master's degree. Imagine walking into a car dealership and meeting a salesman who explains everything about the car you want to buy. Wouldn't it be a slap in the face to offer someone half a car when he has paid for the whole thing? You're convinced that it's a good deal and sign the papers. He gives you the keys and when you get to your car, you're shocked to see that there are no wheels on the car, half of the back seat is gone, and when you look under the hood, there are no wires, hoses, or fluids. Well, if you pay less than the car is worth, don't expect to get all the parts. If you are a church wanting a shiny new car but aren't willing to pay full price for it, don't be surprised if the wheels are gone along with half of the back seat and parts are missing from the engine compartment. If you pay a full-time pastor part-time wages, you'll take away his drive to work hard, his countenance will be reduced, and parts of his ministry will be gone. The pastor should be able to focus on the ministry instead of working hard to pay for the wheels, the back seat, and the parts in his engine compartment. He needs to be paid fairly so his mind won't be divided.

Furthermore, statistics on divorce show that money issues play a very significant role in the reasons couples quarrel; money issues eventually lead many to divorce. Because divorce rates among Christians are practically the same as non-Christians, the church has a duty to do everything to minimize the stresses that precede divorce, especially among ministers and their wives.

If churches are so focused on getting people into heaven but fail to teach practical living such as financial stewardship, then they haven't taught the whole counsel of God. Jim Rickard nailed it when he declared that pastors who struggle financially will hesitate to teach biblical stewardship, a principle every member needs to practice including the leadership of the church. Churches must invest well in their pastors by paying them generously. What would you do if you didn't have to worry about finances and wanted to help people? The possibilities are endless. If you are the Hiring Church, think about it from the candidate's perspective. Resources that can help churches determine a fair salary for pastors include _The Annual Compensation Handbook for Church and Staff_ from Christian Ministry Resources, Zondervan's _2000 Minister's Tax and Financial Guide_ by Dan Busby, and _How to Set Clergy Compensation_ by Steve Clifford.

Your denominational headquarters could tell you what pastors in churches like yours are paid. A typical package includes:

- Base salary
- Benefits: parsonage / housing allowance
- Paid plan: pension plans or contributions to a retirement plan / health insurance (vision & dental) / paid vacations / continuous education / life Insurance
- Reimbursements
- Annual reviews for cost of living increase

Showing on-going concern for the EM pastor's finances will demonstrate to him that the church cares deeply about his well-being. This will increase his longevity and loyalty to the church. Paul Newman responded to the question of why he never divorced Joanne by saying, "Why fool around with hamburger when you have steak at home?" If a church provides adequately for the EM pastor, he won't have to look elsewhere for his needs. And don't forget about encouragement which can go a long way for a pastor. A simple note or card expressing appreciation or having a Pastor Appreciation Day is a great way to show care to a pastor. Yes, money gifts are greatly appreciated, but so is the thought behind it.

We can't afford the median salary for full time pastors.

For the right cause, vision, potential, and experience, ministers are willing to help churches, even if the salary is low.

The Right Cause

Does your church have the right cause? Do you fight for any social injustice? Missionaries, pastors, evangelists, lay people, and those who are willing to sacrifice their own dreams for a cause that is greater than their own are willing to support the organization or the church. Vernon Brewer is the founder and president of World Help, a nonprofit, non-denominational Christian organization uniquely qualified and strategically positioned to meet the spiritual and physical needs of hurting people around the world. Brewer noted, *"I first came face-to-face with the heartbreaking tragedy of AIDS in 1987. I was on a mission trip to Uganda. The devastation was just beginning. Before then, I had only seen news footage or read about the epidemic that was spreading its death grip across the world."* The author continues, *"In recent months, God has placed an overwhelming burden on my heart and in the hearts of every staff member at World Help for the children affected by AIDS – those who have been abandoned and orphaned because of this tragic pandemic."*[18]

A local church was in need of a pastor. They advertised in the clergy directory that they were looking for a conservative pastor who was willing to fight for the cause of the unborn and added that the pay was low. Only a few applied for this position, but the one pastor they invited is now a leader who fights for the rights of the unborn. His passion in life was to fight for the injustice done to unborn children. The church identity matched the pastor's mission, and he was willing to be their pastor even though the pay was low.

The Right Vision

A black preacher with his Korean wife and a white couple started a multicultural church with only a handful of people and one vision. David Anderson set out to build the church of his dreams. Unfortunately, no one seemed to care in the beginning. So, to make ends meet David worked in telemarketing for Craftmatic Adjustable Beds. After leading many people to the Lord, Bridgeway Community Church in Columbia, Maryland was born. What began as a dream became a reality. It took years and countless struggles, but now with a church of 2500 attendees David Anderson is a sought-after speaker and writer on multicultural ministry. Bridgeway Community Church is one of the forerunners of racial reconciliation and helps churches build multicultural bridges in their community.

The Right Potential

The church might not have the necessary funds to hire a new pastor, but with the right vision and potential for growth, many will catch the wave and take the risk. Below is an excerpt from Part 7 Asian Church Models.

> *We invited our pastor and his wife to dinner and shared our vision for a new kind of Korean church where the floundering and slowly dissipating 1.5 and 1st generation Korean Americans can worship in a culturally relevant environment, in a language that could touch their hearts, and where worship was vibrant, dynamic, and open and where they can experience the move of the Holy Spirit with power and freedom. We made a case for starting this new church experiment right here in our city, and asked him to seriously consider this proposition, assuring him of our commitment for ministry partnership and support in this venture, especially with regard to the English service.*
>
> *The rest became history as we launched a new church plant several months later with half a dozen families. It was a very successful launch. After half a year of praying and preparing, the church burst out of the gate running. The inaugural service had over 300 people attending, and month after month, it just kept growing and broke a thousand attendees in the first four years.*
>
> *-   A Lay Leader*

This lay leader had a vision, and the Korean pastor saw the potential. The Holy Spirit brought them together to plant a successful ministry.

The Right Experience

Some churches do not have the means to pay for a part-time minister. In this case they should offer whatever they can to the potential candidate in the hope that he will accept the offer to gain ministry experience. For some ministers gaining experience in the pulpit is worth more than receiving a paycheck. This is the reason many seminary students intern in churches for free, because they relish the opportunity to gain experience. A young white Bible college student accepted an offer to be a youth pastor at a Korean church in Illinois. The part-time salary of $1,000 was barely enough to keep him afloat, but he was willing to take the offer so he could gain some intercultural ministry experience while completing his degree.

The "Return of Loyalty" principle

Each year those who are willing to gamble with their lives try to cross the North Korean border into China. Their goal: reach South Korea, the land of democracy. People of all classes have attempted to escape. Some make it out alive while those who are caught face imprisonment, enslavement, or the worst, death. North Korea has indoctrinated the people with their Communist ideology but lack a fully-devoted nation of followers, mostly because the government's actions proved the opposite. Starvation was rampant and cruelty to the millions who were poor led to a lack of trust in the government. And because loyalty is built on trust, it was scarce in a country that exploited its people. The North Korean government does not care about its people, so its people are looking for a country with a better government.

On the other hand, if the North Korean, communist government actually followed through on their original ideology to support the people and provide for their basic needs (food, clothing, and shelter), then the number of people defecting would be extremely low. The people would return the government's loyalty to the people with sacrificial service to the government. It's human nature to want to return the favor. This is the "return of loyalty" principle.

Similarly, when a church and its leaders show the new pastor their concern for him and his family, even though the salary is low, the natural response for the pastor is to return the favor. So, when times of crisis arise, the pastor will step up to guide the flock through the difficulties. The bond between the pastor and the church will hold together through the challenges of their ministry. In essence, the church will become a part of the pastor's family.

Chapter 17

Small Church, No M

What about small churches that cannot afford to pay at all?

In a typical Asian church finding volunteers is not a difficult task even for a small church. However, finding the right lay leader who can speak English and can relate to the children of the 1st immigrant church is another matter. Young adults or college students are frequently asked to help, and many are willing to volunteer, but as time passes it becomes more difficult for these young people to be consistent. This is the issue that Pastor Nathan Lee experienced, and here is his story:

> In the Washington Metropolitan area alone, there are over 350 Korean American churches, and more than 80 % of churches have less than 50 members. It is close to impossible for an EM pastor to come and work for these churches. What is a small Korean American church to do?

> I was struggling with this issue for last 12 years. We started to have joint youth retreats for small churches that couldn't have their own. However, we were only able to do one retreat a year which didn't seem to impact the students for long term spiritual growth. Most of the youth teachers and college students who

served as small group leaders wanted to have more than just a retreat. We started to have leadership training for youth teachers and college students who had a heart for youth ministry. We met once a month to pray together and invited guest speakers to train us. It developed into a ministry now called "Father's Heart Ministry" (FHM).

Father's Heart Ministry (FHM)

The Father's Heart Ministry is a network of churches in the Del-Mar-Va (Delaware, Maryland and Virginia) region of the United States that is dedicated to serving the Lord Jesus Christ by helping to strengthen its small local churches. The first Father's Heart retreat was held on August 2004 and it was a joint youth retreat consisting of seven local churches in the Del-Mar-Va region. This retreat provided vital support to small local churches, which often have only limited resources, by conducting youth events that would not be otherwise possible. By God's grace and guidance, these local churches united and integrated their efforts, resources and leadership skills, along with support from the Metropolitan Council of Korean Baptist Churches (MCKBC). As a result the churches were able to hold retreats specifically tailored to teenagers attending small churches, which eventually, to the Glory to God, led to salvation and spiritual growth of many young people.

Throughout the years, God has expanded, directed and evolved the FHM's vision in significant ways. As beneficial as the retreats have been for all of us, three important issues remain.

1. While yearly retreats are beneficial, they cannot ensure lasting daily devotion to Christ.

When youth students return home from a retreat, they seem to quickly lose the passion for Christ which they gained and experienced only a short time ago. However, while the leaders were willing to do whatever was necessary to help the youth continue to grow, they realized that:

2. It is the responsibility of the local church, not the para-church to ensure that the youth are being properly discipled in Christ after the retreat.

It is not the place of para-church ministries to take upon themselves the role of discipling youth students directly. Because it is the church and not the para-church that Christ instated, it is the para-church's responsibility to submit to the authority of the local church. However:

3. Small Local Churches often lack the resources to fulfill the responsibility of discipling its youth.

There is a constant outcry in the churches today for effective youth leaders. Too frequently out of desperation, many unqualified older students are forced into positions of leadership with little training and guidance. Furthermore, many youth students today harbor feelings of resentment and bitterness toward their churches as they live through the inevitable struggles of an imperfect church.

The Father's Heart Ministry exists as a network to provide help and support to these local churches. With the discipleship process in order to produce student-leaders in our community, we were able to help these small churches. The Lord Jesus Christ calls us to go and make disciples, and FHM aims to fulfill that mandate.

By sharing our own struggles and weaknesses with one another and through encouragement, teaching, discipleship, perseverance, training, and loving one another, this ministry hopes to bring together churches that are willing to do whatever it takes to build up the body of Christ, in the context of both the local church and the universal Church.

Although our churches are many and diverse in the Del-Mar-Va region, we are all one body in Christ. Father's Heart Ministry seeks to share these concerns with one another, suffering and rejoicing together for the purpose of building the church and honoring our Lord.

There are many organizations that supply man power and resources to help small churches. The majority of them are American; however, organizations like "Father's Heart Ministry" that target small Korean-American churches do exist and are willing to help.

Pastor Lee mentions that one of the reasons the small churches are hesitant to work with one another was the fear of losing their small youth group to another ministry. Trusting that another ministry will not "steal" their children is a challenging hurdle the 1st gen pastors must face.

The majority of the head churches desire to take care of their 2nd gen members and have enthusiastically stated that they are a crucial part of the church's future. However for some, the allotment of finances for hiring an EM pastor is placed either at the middle or bottom of the overall church budget expense. If the 2nd gen is truly essential to the future of the church, then the Head Church needs to reflect that in itsz budget.

From the Heart of an EM Pastor

During my candidating process one of the elders warned me not to ask or mention salary. He stated that if I asked about salary, then I would be perceived as worldly minded and not trusting in God to provide. Although God has blessed me in every way, it was difficult to answer my wife regarding how we would pay the mortgage and other bills. Did we need to sell the house and buy something smaller, and how could we do that in light of the housing market bringing our house under water. It was forbidden to speak about money. This added a lot of stress to the whole process.

At first, the deacons offered $1,500 as a part-time college pastor, but then only gave $1,000. I spoke with the deacons and they said they would fix the problem. The problems continued and each time I approached them they said it would be solved soon. By the fourth month, I had to look for another part-time job, trying to make ends. I didn't let this bother me, but after the fifth time, they said that the original agreement was wrong and there was miscommunication. I settled for $1,200. There was no transparency with the deacons.

Chapter 18

Scripture on Paying Pastors

Does the Bible support pastors receiving a salary?

1 Timothy 5:17-18 (NASB)
[17]The elders who rule well are to be considered worthy of double honor, especially those who work hard at preaching and teaching.
[18]For the Scripture says, "YOU SHALL NOT MUZZLE THE OX WHILE HE IS THRESHING," and "The laborer is worthy of his wages."

As 1 Timothy 5 states pastors who preach and teach are worthy of double honor. It's not honoring to give them less than what their service deserves. The compensation for them should be more than fair. Apostle Paul references Deuteronomy 25:4 and Leviticus 19:13 to remind the people of their duty to support the pastor. In Luke 10:7 Jesus himself taught that servants of God deserve to be paid for their service, and Matthew 10:10 reiterates it.

Luke 10:7
Stay in that house, eating and drinking what they give you; for the laborer is worthy of his wages. Do not keep moving from house to house...

Matthew 10:10
...or a bag for your journey, or even two coats, or sandals, or a staff; for the worker is worthy of his support.

1 Corinthians 9:3-4
³My defense to those who examine me is this:
⁴Do we not have a right to eat and drink?

"Right to eat and drink" is a figurative reference concerning financial support from the congregation to the minister of the gospel. The meaning is typically associated with the right to "eat and drink" at the expense of others. Apostle Paul is saying that he has a legitimate right to receive financial support from the people to whom he was ministering.

1 Corinthians 9:14
So also the Lord directed those who proclaim the gospel to get their living from the gospel.

Apostle Paul is giving the rationale for the pastor's right to receive financial support from the churches he served or is now serving. In verses 7–13 Paul explains why he shouldn't have to work at a trade to earn a living, rather, he should be able to devote his time, focus, and energy to ministering to the flock that God has entrusted to him.

"Who at any time serves as a soldier at his own expense? Who plants a vineyard and does not eat the fruit of it? Or who tends a flock and does not use the milk of the flock?" (1 Cor. 9:7). Apostle Paul points out that soldiers don't pay for their own expenses nor have to raise support in order to serve in the military. It is the government's responsibility to provide for their food, clothing, shelter, and armaments, necessary for their service.

In the analogy about the farmers, *"Or is he speaking altogether for our sake? Yes, for our sake it was written, because the plowman ought to plow in hope, and the thresher to thresh in hope of sharing the crops. If we sowed spiritual things in you, is it too much if we reap material things from you?" (vv 10-11).* He is making the point that the farmer does not cultivate his crops for free. There is the anticipation of enjoying the fruits of his labor. In essence Paul reasons that if he works as a minister of the gospel, he should be able to expect financial compensation- equivalent to wages.

From Jesus to Apostle Paul the Bible is clear that the preacher's service is to be compensated so that the pastor can focus on the ministry.

Proverbs 3:27 (NASB)
Do not withhold good from those to whom it is due,
when it is in your power to do it.

Leviticus 19:13
Do not defraud or rob your neighbor.
Do not hold back the wages of a hired worker overnight.

Questions to Answer:

What are the current salaries of the pastors at your church?

Pastor's name   _____

   Degree Earned   _____

   Current Salary   _____

Pastor's name   _____

   Degree Earned   _____

   Current Salary   _____

Pastor's name   _____

   Degree Earned   _____

   Current Salary   _____

Does the pastor's salary match those of their counterparts as mentioned in this book? Yes _____ No _____

What is the average salary of the pastors in your surrounding area?

Church Name: _____

   $_____

Church Name: _____

$_____

Church Name: _____

$_____

When was the last salary review?

Month _____ Day _____ Year _____

Has your compensation plan been updated? Yes _____ No _____

What is the consideration of the salary for the new EM pastor and why?

Salary from $ _____ to $ _____

Salary is based upon:

_____

_____

_____

_____

Degree Required:

_____

Optional:

_____

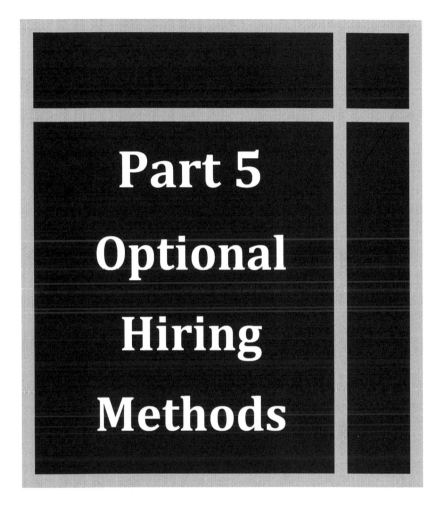

Part 5

Optional

Hiring

Methods

Comparing traditional approaches to hiring an EM pastor with a method that is more comprehensive, highlighted some ways to reduce conflicts before the candidate accepted the position. When a pastor is hired, initially there are some excitements and anticipations that the church will move to next level, but when the joy and excitement whines down, disappointment begins to build in the leaders and congregation members. Silent and unwritten expectations, and unclear goals and objectives become heavy loads for the newly hired pastor.

5
Optional Hiring Methods

Much of the reason for the ambiguity, misunderstanding, and confusion with ministry responsibilities are due to the lack of clarity before the church hires the pastor. This is a common problem in many Korean and other Asian American (AsiAm) churches. The primary objective of this chapter is to reduce the amount of confusion, so that misunderstanding is defused and clear boundaries are set.

As the previous chapters mentioned it is crucial for the church to have an identity. The church needs to know what it is, what its core values are, and what its overarching goal is before continuing on with the hiring process. If the church does not know its own identity, it cannot determine if an individual is the right fit. A pastoral candidate cannot be chosen merely by means of the application, resume, interview, and passion. The church must know what it needs, and it won't know what it needs unless it knows its identity.

Once a church has determined its identity, this information must be placed on its website to attract the right pastor. The majority of the potential EM candidates will learn about the church through its website even before sending in their resumes. Clear and concise information about the identity of the church along with its history will give the potential pastor what he needs in order to consider applying there.

Chapter 19

Vid

Recommendations of Optional Hiring Methods

Doing something different!

Creating a Separate Website for EM

Because EM pastors will research the potential church through its website, the church should provide detailed information for the candidates to view. Along with the church's vision, mission, core values, and goals, a history of the KM church and the EM ministry will aid the candidate in his decision to send a resume. Research of over 50 Korean church websites revealed that less than half had some form of a webpage in English. Even on the websites that had something in English, it was difficult to find the link to the English Ministry page. Without the ability to read Korean it would be difficult for most 2nd gen pastors to find the EM link. If your church does not have an obvious EM link, design one as quickly as possible. Having your own website, separate from KM, will make a significant difference in how the potential EM pastor will view your church. It will really help in your search for a good EM pastor.

ꓹ Presentation

ʌother way to attract a potential EM pastor is to create a video presentation of the congregation members. The direct dialogue of the members explaining why they are in need of an EM pastor will help connect the members to the right candidate. The potential shepherd can connect with the flock even before he visits the church.

Building relationships is one of the key elements of the EM pastor's ministry, so personal contact with the church members through online video can assist the potential minister with his decision to join them. These videos will help the candidate connect with the congregation even before meeting them face to face. Seeing the pictures of the summer picnic is one thing, but seeing and hearing the passion of the EM congregation is heart-warming.

What to have on the EM website?

Along with the explanation of the vision, mission, core values, and goals of the church, the following are recommended features to include:

1. **Brief Church History:** Candidates will find it helpful when churches explain how they were founded, their journey, and where they are headed. An American pastor went to Chicago to be interviewed by an independent church plant of mostly 2nd gen Korean-Americans. He was first attracted by their history and their struggles in building

the foundation of the church. As a former missionary to Asia, he considered the history of the church to be a major factor in his decision to apply.

[Sample]

The first part of 2005 was an exciting time as two churches, Community Church and Christian Church, joined together to form one new church: Christian Community Church. The merger was fueled by a sense of common vision. Back in November 2003, leaders from the Community and Christian churches began meeting on a regular basis to talk and pray about the possibility of God leading our two ministries together. As we shared, we wondered, "Why?" Why change two ministries that have grown strong and found a meaningful niche in the community over the past ten years? Why rock the boat in a city where constant change is an exhausting norm? Over many months, our questions began to change. "Why not was the thought?" Why not bring together two ministries that have such an overlapping, already-shared vision? Why not combine our gifts and resources to harness our different ministry strengths? What would it be like to start a church not from scratch but with deep and rich histories, to bring together not dying but thriving ministries, to submit ourselves to closure for the sake of a new beginning?

In the end, Community campus focus and Christian community orientation were seen as vitally complimentary parts of a unified vision. And we began to dream of a church where students would not only learn about life-long discipleship principles but also rub shoulders with others who were pursuing a relationship with God in contexts very different than theirs, outside of a university setting. We longed for a church where non-student, resident members of our community could share a common life of faith with students. In January 2005 Christian Community Church was birthed out of a belief that people from different walks and stages of life have a great deal to learn from believing, worshiping, and serving God together.

Church Profile: A church profile is helpful to the potential pastor in setting the direction for the church. If the church is looking for a pastor with strong leadership skills, then it should consider a "church profile" to help the potential leader formulate a vision for the church.

[1ˢᵗ Sample: Church Profile]

Our church profile reflects the nature of (City) as a "college town." Within this diverse community, we have established a niche ministering to various groups of Asian-Americans (students, singles, and young families).

Approximate attendance of various ministries

Sunday service: 120 during academic year, 50 during summer.

Weekly small groups: 50 – 70

Vision/(group name) Friday night meetings (University Campus Ministry): 20 – 30

Age of members

3% 0-11   2% 12-18   65% 19-24   30% 25-34

Occupation

20% Professional   80% Other (Students)

Educational level of adults

5% High school   60% college   35% graduate school

Racial/Ethnic composition of congregation

95% Asian   5% Other

Style of liturgy used in worship

Mixture of traditional and contemporary

List of paid staff positions

1 Full-time Senior Pastor

1 Part-time Pastoral Intern

Other Leadership Positions

Fellowship Coordinator

Welcoming Coordinator

Outreach Coordinator

[2nd Sample: Church Profile]

Young Adults Ministry Pastor

Job Description:

(Church Name) is a church of approximately 2,400+ in attendance on the weekends. We currently have four different services in (City). One of the services is a gathering predominantly composed of 18-35 year olds called 'Fusion.' Fusion was started in October 2004 and since then has grown to an average of 525 young adults and children. There are approximately 30 Fusion life groups that gather throughout the week. We are looking for someone to become the lead pastor for Fusion. This person must have a heart to lead spiritually convinced and unconvinced young adults to complete commitment to Jesus Christ.

FAQs:

--Why is there an opening for something that is going well?
The current Fusion pastor is becoming the co-lead pastor of the entire church.

--Will I have any staff help in leading Fusion?
Yes. Currently the Fusion staff includes three life group pastors, an event coordinator, a worship leader and an

administrative assistant in addition to the lead pastor for Fusion.

--Where can I learn more about (Church name) and Fusion?

(Church website) or visit in person.

--Will I be able to afford a living?

Yes. The position is full time plus health, dental, and retirement benefits. Salary is commensurate with experience.

--Timeline?

We are going to keep looking until we find the right person. If you are reading this, that means we are most likely still looking!

INTERESTED?

Submit your resume and we'll go from there.

2. **Description of the Area:** If the potential pastor is from another state and has a negative perception of your state, he will rule out your state automatically. A pastor friend with an aversion to cold and snow crossed out any churches in the Mid-west states. He wouldn't even consider going there. On the other hand a church from the Mid-west did such an excellent job of describing the local area and its attractions that I thought that I was looking at the travel channel. This particular church was looking for a pastor with a family who could connect to a growing body of young families. So most of their descriptions of the area primarily featured what

189

families could do together. Because EM pastors place their families on top of their priority list, advertising local family-friendly ventures was a great idea.

[Sample]

Dear Prospective Candidate applying for the position of Executive Pastor,

We value your interest. (Church name) is a growing, evangelical, multi-campus church of about 900 on Sunday mornings. (Church name) growth and expansion to multi-campuses has accelerated the pace, and stretched the responsibilities of the staff. This new position of Executive Pastor was created to bring a more sophisticated level of process and organization, and free up our Senior Pastor from the responsibilities of the day-to-day church operation.

Our two campuses are located in the affluent suburbs of the north shore of beautiful (state). We are 20 miles from both (state) and great ocean beaches. (Name of) counties take pride in excellent school systems, yet at the same time we live among the largest un-churched population in the United States.

This is an exciting time to join our team. God has blessed us with a high quality ministry and support staff and an ever-growing congregation. We are seeking a person who can complement and work closely with the Senior Pastor and the Elder Board to implement the church vision.

Decreasing Ambiguity, Misunderstanding, and Confusion

As the researchers Jin Han and Cameron Lee indentified, the greatest indicators of stress among Korean American pastors are the boundary ambiguity and presumptive expectations. In order to reduce these, the information should be placed on the website clearly visible to all who are interested in the position. By placing the descriptions online for the potential pastors to review, the church is giving them a mental image of its daily operations.

> Churches can dramatically decrease boundary ambiguity and presumptive expectations by initially stating a clear and thorough description of the responsibility and role of the hiring pastor.

The following is an example from a church that understands the importance of setting boundaries and clarifying expectations.

[Sample of the Responsibilities of an Executive or Administrative Pastor]

Staff Responsibilities

1. Individual Meetings. The Executive Pastor is responsible to meet individually on a regular basis with each of the full-time staff that report directly to him.

2. Staff Meetings. The Executive Pastor is responsible to plan, lead, and conduct all staff meetings with the staff team who report directly to him. This meeting can be either weekly or as needed. He should also help implement team meetings for other staff with their direct supervisors.

3. Leadership and Coaching. The Executive Pastor is to schedule individual time, and group training when needed to help develop and coach each staff member for leadership and ministry development. It is important to visit each staff's ministry periodically and provide them the necessary support and oversight they need to do their jobs.

4. Staff Care. The Executive Pastor is to shepherd each staff and their families by creating an environment of care. The Executive Pastor must care for any staff needs that they may have by ministering to them through pastoral care, counseling, or other avenues. It is important to shepherd those you lead.

5. Staff Communication. The Executive Pastor is to facilitate communication & conflict management for the individual staff member and staff team. It is up to the Executive Pastor to communicate to the staff, and let them know what is expected of them, and how they are to communicate with the Executive Pastor and each other.

6. Staff Accountability. Excluding the Senior Pastor, the Executive Pastor is to hold all the staff accountable in their budget spending, time usage, job performance, personal purity (if it is a cross gender situation it is necessary to make sure they have someone they are accountable to regarding the intimate issues of their lives), personal devotions, and personal and professional relationships. He should also help them establish individual and ministry goals consistent with the church goals and vision.

7. Personnel. The Executive Pastor is responsible for recommending staff to be hired, disciplined or dismissed to the Senior Pastor for all positions. The Executive Pastor is responsible for making a recommendation for positions available if (church name) is looking to hire for any position. The Elder Board may elect to authorize a search committee to be chaired by the Executive Pastor.

8. Personnel File. The Executive Pastor is responsible to review regularly each staff's individual personnel file and their job description. The Executive pastor will approve vacation requests and track vacation days/sick days for the staff and make recommendations for salary adjustments to the Senior Pastor and Elders.

9. Volunteerism. The Executive Pastor leading by example is to nurture volunteerism for the staff and congregation.

Ministry Development & Strategy Responsibilities

1. Volunteer Leadership. The Executive Pastor is responsible for holding each staff member accountable for living out, implementing and developing healthy volunteer leaders and measuring the efficiency and effectiveness of all ministries.

2. Oversee an Annual Church Review Process. The Executive Pastor is responsible for performing a yearly review of every ministry in the church and overall church strategy and direction and presenting this report annually to the Pastoral Team and Elders.

3. Reviews. The Executive Pastor is responsible for performing the reviews & evaluations of all staff members who report directly to him. This will be done on an annual basis (or more frequently as needed). He will present annual goals for the following year. He should also participate in the review of staff under the supervision of other staff and approve the review.

4. Ministry Budgets. The Executive Pastor is responsible for overseeing the development and implementation of each ministry's budget. The Executive Pastor will serve as the chair of the Finance Committee responsible for establishing financial policies and budgets on the Elder board's behalf. The Executive Pastor is to hold the staff accountable in their budget spending.

5. Strategic Planning and Implementation. The Executive Pastor will meet regularly with the Senior Pastor to clarify vision and develop action plans. He will ensure that strategic planning is an ongoing process, appointing others to help as necessary. He will assist the Senior Pastor in communicating these strategic plans with the Elders.

Responsibilities to the Elder Board

1. To assist the Senior Pastor in giving direction through establishing and clearly communicating vision, goals, and plans to pastoral and office staff.

2. To ensure that the Board's decisions or stipulations are followed in the operational services of the church.

3. To facilitate the flow of information to and from the Elder Board and provide current information to the Board to aid in their decision making.

4. To attend the Elder Board meetings but will not vote.

Why do you have to be so specific? What does the Bible say?

Can you imagine God telling Noah to build an ark and not telling him how? "Noah, I want you to build an ark for me and you figure it out, just be moved by the Holy Spirit and He will guide you" is NOT what God said to Noah. God was specific in the design, size, cargo space, and even the hole in the roof. *"Make a roof for it and finish the ark to within 18 inches of the top . . ."* (Gen. 6:16) is a specific command from God. Only a sovereign God would know why the ark would need such a hole. It is estimated by scholars that the ark could have measured between 437 to 512 feet in length and with this size, I would have told Noah to put at least 30 feet of "Sun roof" at the top instead of 18 inches. It's a good thing I don't help anyone in construction for I would've failed miserably.

And I thought only lawyers cared about personal injury; God cares about the details even more. Exodus 21:12-36 gives us the specifics of what to do in many different scenarios of personal injury, but who would have ever thought to include this? *"If men who are fighting hit a pregnant woman and she gives birth prematurely but there is no serious injury, the offender must be fined whatever the woman's husband demands and the court allows . . ."* (Ex. 21:22).

If you really want to know whether God cares about the details, look at a snowflake under a microscope. Even before the microscope was invented, God detailed the making of a snowflake. Even before we realized its intricacy and beauty or could appreciate it, it was part of His design. If leadership is important to God, should we not put the time and effort into making the position clear? From the detailed description of the tabernacle to the occupation of the Promised Land and from Solomon's building the Temple to Nehemiah's rebuilding of the walls around Jerusalem, if they didn't have the details, they would have been lost trying to obey the Lord. Why would it be any different with the church outlining the specifics of hiring a new pastor or staff? The details helped Noah understand his boundaries and what was expected of him, and the details will make clear the position the church is trying to fill and practically eliminate the boundary ambiguity and presumptive expectations that exist in ministry situations.

Chapter 20

Questions?

What questions should you ask?

2nd Round: Questionnaire

Once the church receives a fair number of applications via its website, it must review them to narrow down the search. After pouring through the details of the candidates' backgrounds, more questions need to be asked. This is the "2nd Round" of the search proceedings. The following is an example of the type of questions that can be asked in the 2nd Round. Do you have any experience in the Asian-American church context? If yes, please explain. Direct and specific questions will move the church closer toward the best match.

[Sample: Lead Pastor]

Direction: Interested applicants should send their information via email to be considered for this review process.

Questionnaire:

1. What about (Your Church Name) and (Job Title) specifically attracted you to send us your resume?

2. What are your top 5 strengths as defined by the Strengths Finder Tool (Other strength finding tools can be used)?

3. What is/are your top spiritual gift(s)? List no more than 3 gifts in order of strength.

4. We like to use a tool called the DISC Inventory in assessing our potential staff. If you are familiar with your DISC profile, please put an "x" by which letter most matches your personality. If not, please take the DISC online (it is offered by any numerous sites). Google in the words: DISC Inventory and send us your profile report.

5. Why are you considering a change to a new position?

6. Where did you last work or what is your currently employment situation? (May we contact your current (or previous) supervisor or employer with questions relating to this search process? If so, please provide the name and contact number of the individual from your current or most recent place of employment.

7. What has been your greatest failure in ministry and/or life?

8. What has been your greatest win or victory in ministry and/or life?

9. What are your financial expectations/needs? (Please be specific.)

[For more samples please refer to Appendix B]

How do you respond once you receive the questions?

The following are some basic examples of replies through email:

Thanks for your interest in our (Position) of (Church Name). We have received your information and will be in touch with you. We anticipate beginning the interview process in mid to late (Date).

Blessings,

Church Name
(Director/Secretary/Coordinator/Pastor Name)

Thank you for your interest in our (position). We have received your resume and forwarded it to our Search team. If they require further information, we will contact you with the request.

Have a blessed day.

(Representative Name)
(Church Name)

Application Rejection:

Thank you for your interest in the (Position) of (Church Name).

Thank you for the time and attention you granted us in submitting your resume and answering our questions. Regrettably, we have not chosen your application to continue in the search procedure. It was a pleasure getting to know you though and wish you the very best in your search for a compatible ministry position.

Sincerely,

(Church Name)
(Representative Name)

3rd Round: Questions to Ask

After the Search Committee has made its selection and the pastoral candidate has made a tentative agreement to come to the church, the final stage of the hiring process remains: confirmation. During the confirmation stage details get clarified even more and final-stage questions are asked. In order to decrease the amount of ambiguity, confusion, and misunderstanding of expectations, ask the following series of questions for the long-term benefit of both parties.

What should the pastor know?

Supervisor: The pastor needs to know who his supervisor is and the person he should report to. In most cases the primary person supervising the EM pastor is the senior KM pastor. In some large Asian churches this may different, but it would be rare.

Performance Reviews: Asian churches do not typically have performance reviews. Annual performance reviews will confirm that the pastor is on track with the church's goals and bring up any concerns that the leadership or church has concerning his performance. It is also a time for the pastor to voice his thoughts on how things are going and what difficulties he may be facing. The exact date of the performance review should be set at the beginning of the pastor's term, and someone who is not the supervisor of the EM pastor should give him the feedback. That is not to say that the senior. pastor won't speak to the EM pastor. They should have their own conversation in addition to the performance review. The performance reviews are based on the detailed responsibilities the church described on their website. **The performance review is not a "critical" evaluation of the pastor (although it should be as detailed as possible) but a time of encouragement for things done well and for creative improvement in areas that didn't fully meet the requirements of the position.** If we are to have an effective ministry, we need to hear how our ministry is being received. Refer to appendix C for a sample "Performance Evaluation" Form.

Termination: The pastor should understand from the beginning what the terms are for his termination. If he consistently underperforms in his duties, he should be the one to remove himself from the position. For one reason or another if he is reluctant, then the church should step in to follow the protocol for his resignation so that the church will have adequate time to find a new pastor. If the termination was due to performance is one thing, but if it was due to immorality or a major conflict, then those issues should be thoroughly addressed before the pastor's departure. Any unresolved conflict will resurface possibly doing more damage than it did before. If the cycle continues, there will be on-going damage to the body. As much as humanly possible, the issues that caused the conflict should be totally resolved. If no policy for termination is written, the church should have one in place before hiring their next pastor. Without a written policy, the church will be scrambling to determine what to do in the midst of the turmoil. Good decisions are hard to make during a state of desperation and heightened emotions.

Vacation and Study Leave: The number of days given for vacation, sickness, and emergencies should be clarified at the time of hiring. The Hiring Church needs to explain the vacation procedures for the first year and adjustments for subsequent years. Vacation time may be 3 weeks for the first year, 4 weeks for the next 3 years, and 6 weeks after four years or more. It should also be explained how to use them. For instance, what does "four weeks of vacation" mean? Can vacation time be taken all at once, or should it be spread out? The clarification on simple things as these can save some frustration in the future. Likewise, communication about continuing education also needs to be discussed or stipulated. Although sabbaticals might not be in the picture at this point, letting the pastor know that a sabbatical is included after five, six, or seven years of service will give the new candidate some hope of a respite, which will be energizing as he begins his ministry for the long hull.

Salary: The salary is what the pastor and his family must live on. The reimbursements for ministry expenses must be kept separately. For most churches the salary is tied closely to the housing allowance, so it is best to discuss the details of the compensation package together. There must be an annual salary review. Nowadays, the economy fluctuates even during the year. The living expense after one year may go up more than the anticipated 3.5%. If the salary review only happens every 2 to 3 years, the pastor will experience unnecessary financial stress before his income is adjusted. In many cases an increase will be needed when the pastor adds an additional family member. Other items that need to be included in the salary package are retirement plans, health insurance, disability insurance, and life insurance.

Moving Costs: The church should have prepared the full estimate cost of a potential move for the candidate. This shows the pastor that the church is serious in making the right investment toward a long-term relationship. By caring for the pastor's need in this area, the church is showing that the pastor does not have to think about any financial aspects of his ministry at the church because the church is taking care of it.

Questions the candidate should ask the hiring committee?

The candidating interview is the best time to discuss the church's expectations and the pastor's role. The church has the protocol of asking the questions first, and afterwards solicit questions from the candidate. Below is a list of possible questions the potential candidate can ask. The questions should be prepared in advance and modified during the interview.

Identity of the Church: If the church does not have a solid vision, mission, core values, and an overarching goal, then it would be appropriate for the pastor to ask questions in regard to the talents, interests, and commitments of the church.

Question: "Why am I of interest to this church?" It is good to know why they are considering the candidate.

Question: "What has been the most significant event in the life of this church since its inception?" The question serves two purposes: We discover what events are significant to the church and what ministries this congregation considers significant.

Question: "What has been the most troubling experience for the life of this church?" This question allows the church members to voice their pain openly. It also informs the pastor what is likely to upset the congregation in the years ahead. Years ago a pastor friend asked a church this question. The church had some confusion about the doctrine of healing and was not exactly sure where the previous pastor stood. In the beginning of their ministry he was conservative in his preaching but later emphasized the doctrine of healing. Because the pastor had not discussed this with the leadership of the church before he began his new practice, there were some uneasy feelings in the church leadership. My friend then asked where they stood on the discussion now. Although the leadership hadn't made up its mind, they were opened to discussing it. The new candidate believed in modern-day healing, so gradually he added sessions of healing whenever he felt the leading of the Spirit. It worked out for everyone. Because the pastor was able to ask these questions from the beginning, he was able to continue the discussion and eventually win them over to the practice.

Question: "What areas of concern need to be addressed by this congregation?" This question is posed to the committee members in order to bring up resolved issues, possibly with the previous pastor. In many cases the conflict with the previous pastor carries over to the new pastor if things weren't reconciled. The congregation may be suspicious of the new pastor because of the way the previous pastor acted. Making sure that the image of the previous pastor does not follow the new pastor is the candidate's responsibility.

Question: "Has the previous pastor's family taken an active role in this church, especially his wife?" Many Asian and especially Korean churches will automatically assume that the pastor's wife will take part in some type of ministry. By asking this question, the committee members will reveal how they felt about the previous pastor's family. Therein lay the criteria by which the new pastor's family will be judged. Then, the pastor should go home to discuss with his wife her thoughts regarding this matter. If the pastor's wife has no calling to serve but is pressured by the church to do so, conflicts in the personal life of the pastor will eventually lead the family to part with the church. This is surfacing unexpressed expectations.

Question: "Is the congregation able to assume the cost of the move, including the cost of the moving insurance?" If this detail is not clarified from the very beginning, the candidate may be presuming on the congregation to provide or not realize that he doesn't have to pay for the move and deal needlessly with the financial stress of the move. Relocating is stressful enough, but having to deal with the financial burden will only make it worse.

Question: "Will the church provide salary and benefits along with health coverage during the move itself?" Normally a move of over 100 miles might take more than just a few days. The new congregation's willingness to begin salary on the day of the move itself will demonstrate care for the pastor. Other questions should be asked to clarify the pastor's compensation package. For further readings on pastors' salaries go to Part 4 Pastor's Salary.

Question: "Is the church willing to put everything in writing so there is no misunderstanding?" In many situations lay leaders, elders, board members and/or deacons will have a rotation term of service. All things discussed with the pastor form the original agreement. Issues may arise when new members who are not familiar with the original discussion will start to bring up issues that were already clarified in the beginning. Putting all that was said in writing will preclude any assumptions about what was intended so that no misunderstanding can occur in these matters. If the head church is not willing to put it in writing or cannot find anyone to do so, then the EM pastor should volunteer to put it in writing for them. There are many incidences where an agreement was made in the beginning, but when a change occurred in the senior leadership and some elders transitioned out, the EM pastor's original agreement was forgotten because there was nothing in writing.

Chapter 21

Starting Your New Ministry

How do you approach the new church?

Dr. Chong came into the new church with much fanfare. His first sermon message was powerful and his exegetical style was sublime. Everyone chatted with him for a bit after the service and went on their individual ways. Pastor Chong moved aggressively and on the following Sunday he announced exciting new events and programs to come. However, as he peered out into the audience, not too many people seemed excited about what he was doing. He let it go, thinking, "This must be normal for this congregation." Then again he preached a strong biblical sermon, this time on Leviticus. Dr. Chong gave his best and applied all that he knew from his seminary education.

During one of the meetings, Dr. Chong asked the leaders, if there were any concerns from the congregation. All the leaders shook their heads, but the following Sunday Dr. Chong found out it wasn't so. He had some abdominal issues and went to the restroom before his message began. There, he overheard a conversation between two members that changed his perspective about his new church. "The new pastor is a nice pastor," said one person. "Yeah, he sure knows the Bible!" said the other. But the comment that struck him was, "He sure knows the Bible, but he sure doesn't know us." Dr. Chong realized that he was preaching to people that he didn't get to know. He met the people here and there and spoke with them superficially, but he didn't truly know the heart of his flock.

A Different Strategy

The next day, Dr. Chong called his good friend who was a consultant for a large firm and sought his advice on how to build a relationship with the people. With his friend's advice absorbed, he took it to the Lord in prayer for confirmation. God confirmed the strategy on how to become a more effective and successful ministry leader. He asked the leaders to set aside a budget for other pastors to come and speak at the church for one month. He told his leaders his objective and why this was important for the church and his longevity there. They agreed.

The next Sunday the church had a guest speaker and Dr. Chong was present and greeting people at the door. He greeted everyone with a big smile and even got to know who the guests were. He even went as far as going to the parking lot to see how people were coming in and out and how the children were being checked in. During the guest speaker's message, he roamed the church with pen and paper taking as many notes as possible. He looked into the children's classes for a brief moment and then headed up to the youth department to see how things were done there. The small youth group was shocked to see the Lead Pastor come in and sit with them. He listened to the part-time youth pastor and chatted briefly with some of the kids. All this time he was taking notes and making an effort to learn the kids' names. During that month he took each of the core leaders out for lunch. He asked questions such as, "What was the previous pastor like? How was his sermon and did it have any impact on the congregation? How well did you know him on a personal basis? What is your honest opinion about him in regard to his strengths and his weaknesses? If there was one priority that our church needs to change, what would it be and why?" Each one of them gave him their honest opinion. What Dr. Chong realized was that the previous pastor's sermons were just like his. He even gave a strong exegetical message on Leviticus. People didn't see any difference between him and the other pastor. Dr. Chong didn't have to wonder why some of his core team members were falling asleep during his messages.

He decided to probe further by asking, "What worked in regard to spiritual growth of the church in the past? What didn't work and why? If you had to start all over, how would you do it differently and why? If you were to create your own church, what would it look like? What is your greatest desire as a Christian? How can I pray for you?" By the end of the month Dr. Chong began to really understand his flock and the desires of their hearts.

The pastor took action and made some changes, including his style of preaching. He had misunderstood the leaders from the beginning when they were requesting a "strong Christ-centered message." To him that meant exegetical in style, but they desired a Christ-centered, transforming, and relevant message concerning their unique situation. By asking them personal questions, Dr. Chong was able to understand their needs and work out a specialized worship service with the worship leader doing things a little differently. Prayer sessions were added toward the end of service and on Tuesday evenings. Personal time with volunteers, teachers, and leaders were scheduled once a month to just enjoy fellowship and grow together through accountability and transparency. Over time ministries evolved, such as a prayer and greeter's ministry.

The bond between the shepherd and the flock grew strong by the year's end. The church started to grow. Dr. Chong realized that if he had taken the time to actually study the people he was shepherding, he could have reduced some stress and sleepless nights. Thankfully, he was still able to realize his blindness before he followed in the footsteps of the previous pastor.

Overarching Goal

Before a pastor begins his new ministry, he should ask for at least a full month, to interview, survey, and understand the congregation before stepping up on the podium to preach. Most pastoral search committees desire their pastors to preach effective biblical messages. But caring for and getting to know the congregation is equally important. People have to be willing to follow the leader and not just attend Sunday service. They need to have the desire to be part of the ministry. This can only happen if the leader shows that he cares and understands the people that he is leading.

For the first year the pastor is encouraged to work on an overarching goal. Some pastors will state, "My overarching goal for this year is to build relationships" or "My overarching goal for this year is building small groups." Not all pastors are extroverts and have the skills to build relationships. Some might be introverts who are not good at one-on-one relationship building, but do well in public speaking. The overarching goal for this particular pastor might be, "My overarching goal for this year is establishing prayer with the core team members once a week." Introverted pastors might not be comfortable relating one-on-one, but they can get to know people by praying for them. Prayer meetings are a great relationship building tool.

The overarching goal for the first year is primarily to understand the flock and connect with them on a deeper level. This is the way to get to know their needs. Whether the church is Asian or American, every member of the congregation needs to feel a sense of community and significance. An effective team ministry begins with relationships. When the relationship with the pastor is strong and trust is built, the congregation will follow him. This the way we all live. We don't follow anyone we don't trust.

For part-time EM pastors, building relationships with the church members is one of the hardest aspects of ministry, primarily because of the time constraints. Remember, if he is to put into his Sunday sermon 16 hours of preparation, he only has 4 hours left in the week to prepare the Bible study he leads and build relationship with his flock. Trying to juggle ministry, seminary, and a part-time job leaves no time for building relationships. With that in mind in order to maximize the little time that's left for all the other aspects of ministry, the pastor must live by purpose. What is the Lord's specific purpose for the church and what role should does the part-time pastor have? Until the church is ready for a full-time EM pastor, the Lord will orchestrate all the details of ministry along the way, including what the part-time pastor should do with the limited time he has.

Church Research

Below are some practical guidelines to help the pastor begin his new ministry year: Make sure to communicate your objectives to the ministry and church leaders. It is always better to over-communicate than to under-communicate. Long-term support is obtained when everyone is kept informed of the destination (goal) and the journey (process).

1. No changes are recommended in the first year. It would be best to attend all the church events at least once to learn from your congregation what is valued. While focusing on preaching every Sunday, the rest of the week should be scheduled for getting to know the church culture and its people. Learning as much about the people as possible will become even more valuable when the process of building a team begins.

2. During this time questions should be asked to help strategize for the future. The questions are asked not for the purpose of learning what to do and not to do. Rather, in asking these questions so much is learned about the people who answer them in the way they answer them. Below are some sample questions that will help kick start this process.

    a. What worked in the past and how did it work?

    b. What didn't work in the past and why?

    c. When new families come, how are the children directed to their classes?

    d. How are people greeted as they enter?

    e. Is there a parking issue?

    f. How do we help the guest after service?

    g. How do we get the family/individual connected?

    *More questions from Dr. Chong's story

3. Invite people to "Evenings with the pastor" (with permission from your spouse). This gathering will be informal and a good way to establish fellowship for future ministry ventures. After all, many of those types of gatherings are soon to take place when ministry is in full swing. As I invited congregation members of all age groups for dinner, I learned much more about them than when I had Bible study with them. In a relaxed atmosphere more of the "real" person comes out.

Visiting core members at work and actually paying for their lunch builds rapport. In the Asian culture the congregation members typically pay for the meal, but I would strongly suggest that the pastor pay for at least the first meal. When the minister pays, it shows humility and takes the financial burden off the member. Often visiting our team members' home, school, or work place can help the pastor identify with them in their world.

Sample Research Application

When I first came on board a large American church, I did a detailed analysis of the pillars of the church. Not key individuals but ministries that supported the primary function of the church. Examples of ministry pillars are children, youth, men's, and women's ministries. And as our church grew we needed to add another pillar. One of the pillars that was missing in this church was the young adults ministry. There was a singles ministry, but it primarily consisted of ages 45 to 55.

1. My first response was to study the congregation and determine the makeup for a potential young adults ministry.

2. I spoke with over 10 young adults in their 20s and 30s to see what their thoughts were about a potential ministry just for them.

3. I then spoke with the leadership team who had been at the church for a longer time to see if in the past there was a young adults ministry and the name of the person who was in charge of it. I discovered from the interviews that a young adults ministry did exist and the person who was in charge then was still present at the church.

4. I interviewed the person who used to run that ministry and gathered pertinent information like why they started it in the first place, how they promoted it, what worked, what didn't work, and why this ministry ended.

5. Then I decided to contact three churches that were similar in culture and context to find out if they had a young adults ministry. From the five an evaluation was done to determine the size of the young adult groups and the congregation. I began first with a phone interview of a small young adult group. Then did a personal interview on a mid-size group that had a congregation size of over 2,000 people. The third group consisted of over 5,000 people. This was strategic to understand what the young adults ministry would look like in three to five years.

6. The following is the actual research for the young adults ministry:

   Overarching Goal: Come up with the best scenario of what the young adults ministry would look like in the beginning, growing, and maturing stages. Three churches that would most resemble the dynamics, environment, and structure of (Church Name) were studied. The following three churches were chosen: (Church 1), (Church 2), and (Church 3). Go to Appendix E for the results.

Questions to Answer:

Do you have your own website?

Yes _____ No _____ (please explain why not)

_____

_____

_____

Do you have any video presentations? Yes _____ No _____

Other _____

Do you know your church history? Yes _____ No _____

What is your church profile? Our church profile is:

_____

_____

_____

_____

_____

What questions are crucial to ask in the 2nd round?

1. _____

2. _____

3. _____

4. _____

5. _____

6. _____

7. _____

8. _____

9. _____

10. _____

Do you agree with the 3rd round of questions? Yes _____ No _____

If you were to re-start your ministry, what would you do differently as a leader?

_____

_____

_____

_____

_____

_____

_____

_____

_____

_____

_____

_____

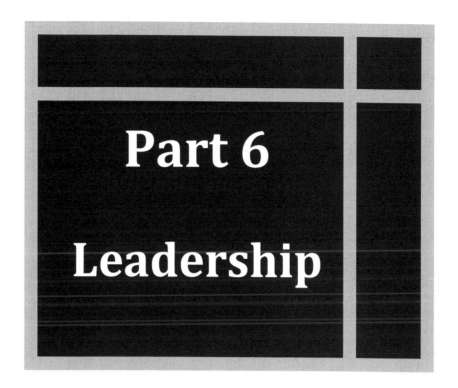

Part 6

Leadership

6

Leadership

When I was in seminary, I met many Koreans who came to the U.S. to get their Master of Divinity degree. My new friend Kim Jae Yong had already received his Master of Divinity from Korea. In fact almost all the 1st immigrant Koreans at my seminary had their Master of Divinity degrees from Korea. I was confused so I asked, "Why are you pursuing an MDiv here in the U.S. when you already have an MDiv from Korea?" He explained that in order for him to get ministry experience in Korea he would have to acquire some additional seminary degree in the U.S. He stressed that many churches in Korea will not even consider a job application if they do not clearly show the additional degree from U.S. He further emphasized that a seminarian would have a better chance at getting hired if he had an additional doctorate or a PhD from the U.S or England.

Academic achievement is a core value in Asian cultures, and Asian immigrant churches keep the value alive by demanding in their leadership higher or multiple degrees. In this aspect of their work ethic, the first gen pastors deserve a great deal of credit. They not only have to complete a degree from Korea, but have to relocate to the U.S. and using a second language obtain another degree while living in a culture not their own. I don't know very many 2nd gen pastors who have written a thesis in a foreign language, and yet that's what many 1st gen pastors have done.

After the rigors of two degrees, ministry should be less stressful-might be the tempting thought. On the contrary as mentioned before 1st gen Korean pastors wear multiple hats and keep long hours serving their members. Consider the early morning prayer which begins at 5:30am and ends anywhere between 6:30-7am. Including travel time, it is a commitment of two and half hours per day totaling 12.5 hours per week. This is on top of the normal office hours they hold beginning at 9am. Add to that the visitations 1 to 2 times per week, and it becomes clear that ministry does not give them a breathing space from the stressful days of pursuing multiple degrees.

Not mentioned was the reality that they too want a familiar and comfortable environment in which to live and raise their children. But they must raise their children while shepherding their flock. They must teach their children two cultures, two languages, and two ways of life, while emphasizing one Christianity. How much pressure can one person actually face? Paul faced a similar level of stress and expressed it this way:

> I have worked much harder, been in prison more frequently, been flogged more severely, and been exposed to death again and again. [24] Five times I received from the Jews the forty lashes minus one. [25] Three times I was beaten with rods, once I was pelted with stones, three times I was shipwrecked, I spent a night and a day in the open sea, [26] I have been constantly on the move. I have been in danger from rivers, in danger from bandits, in danger from my fellow Jews, in danger from Gentiles; in danger in the city, in danger in the country, in danger at sea; and in danger from false believers. [27] I have labored and toiled and have often gone without sleep; I have known hunger and thirst and have often gone without food; I have been cold and naked. [28] Besides everything else, I face daily the pressure of my

concern for all the churches. [29] Who is weak, and I do not feel weak? Who is led into sin, and I do not inwardly burn? (2 Cor 11:23-29)

One thing that can be learned from the brutal schedule that the 1st gen pastors keep is that they really care for their flock. There is no doubt about their commitment to the Lord and His people.

Chapter 22

Asian Church Leadership

Are you willing to follow?

Majority of the 1st gen Korean pastors have fulfilled the mandatory military service where hierarchy was a way of life. This system demands respect for authority. Within the 1st gen mindset, when an authority figure gives a command, it is as good as done. In the 2nd gen mindset, he gets to choose to obey or not. Therein, lie some of the issues of conflict between 1st gen leaders and EM pastors. The answer lies not just in the lack of military service, but the culture and background of the 2nd gen pastor. As latchkey children who were rarely given words of encouragement, they resented authority beginning with their parents. The children pretty much raised themselves while their parents were busy working long hours in order to over-provide for them. The only kind of authority came in the form of commands to do their homework and finish their chores. With little time spent together the children received very little accountability; they went astray finding support from their peers who were independent thinkers in a me-oriented society. "I want to do it my way," has been cultivated into their psyche because it was a way of life. So, while the 1st gen leaders are saying, "When I say jump!" you say, "How high?" the 2nd gen pastors are saying, "Let me do it my way." Thus, the culture clash in ministry philosophy becomes one of the highest reasons of tension.

Traditional Asian Family Dynamics

To better understand the Asian leadership structure, we must first understand the culture of the 1st gen traditional Asian family and the dynamics of assimilating into the American system.

Hierarchical: Korean, Chinese, Japanese and other nations have similar styles, males and older individuals hold the authority. And respect is built into the system. In the Korean culture there are four terms for older sibling. Depending on whether the younger sibling is male or female, male and female older siblings are called by different names. A younger brother calls an older brother as "hyong," but he calls his older sister "nuna." A younger sister calling her older brother uses "opah," but calls her older sister by "unni." So, if another Korean outside the family hears the terms being used, he knows exactly what the relationship is. Hierarchy is built into the language. And calling my older sibling by his first name is very disrespectful in the traditional Korean culture. I once called my third brother by his first name because I got angry with him, and my oldest brother slapped me upside the head. Knowing your hierarchical order is important for survival.

Gender Differences: Traditionally, males are highly valued in the Asian culture because they carry on the family name. Even today in many parts of Asia when it comes to babies, females are aborted until a male is conceived. The role of the female is to be passive and adhere to the husband's side of the family. She must be subservient to her husband, perform domestic duties, and bear children. The role of the male is to provide for the family and maintain command

225

of his household. Though times are changing throughout Asia, this particular model is still sustained.

Respect: The entire culture revolves around the theme of respect. Respect for ancestors, the elderly, and authoritative figures are woven into the society. Even in the languages not only is there special terms for older siblings, but there is formal and informal levels of communication. As a matter of fact, Korean has four levels of communication. The highest is the language used to speak to royalty, and the lowest is what the royalty uses to speak to the peasants. It won't be hard to guess which level an older sibling uses with his younger sibling, the same one used by the parents with their children. Think of a household as a mini-kingdom. There is the king (father), the queen (mother), and their subjects (children).

Communication: Traditionally, the father communicates his desires to the family, and the wishes of the father become the priority of the family. And there is no such thing as back-talking. Centuries ago in Asia, back-talkers were severely punished, imprisoned, and even executed. In many traditional homes, the children will ask questions to the mother instead of the father, then, in turn the mother will ask the father and give the answer to her children.

Family: Children learn early in life that the family is central and its image supreme. Any marring of the family image will bring shame so it is a carefully guarded pursuit. This is why problems in the family are not readily divulged. Unlike the father who brought the demonized boy to the Lord in Matthew 17, the Korean parents will ask Jesus to come to their home for ministry in order to avoid shame.

Discipline: The father primarily dispenses discipline for misbehaviors. It was and still is a very common practice in the Asian culture. When a family member shows a bad reflection on the kin, the family and the individual will typically go through shame and guilt. Moreover, shame and guilt can also be used to control and discipline. Although toned down some because of the way American society views it, it is not going to disappear anytime soon.

Loyalty and Honor: Early on children are taught the importance of loyalty to the family, and whatever brings honorable to the family is valued. This is the reason family issues are hidden from the public and handled within. Although the law requires the reporting of sexual abuse, the Asian community will hardly obey the law since it will bring dishonor to the family to make it public. Mental illness is sign of weakness, so it too will be hidden. Asian parents structure their children's lives for academic success because it is the most publicly honored pursuit.

Emotions: Traditionally, displaying minimal emotions are a sign of maturity and self-control. Showing affection is a cultural taboo. Until recently, not even teenagers of opposite sex held hands in public.

Father: Is typically more authoritative and distant, focusing on career or business and less emotionally demonstrative and involved. The father will focus on the provisions of the family's economical and physical needs. Care is shown by supplying the physical needs of the family. I (Jae) never even saw my father kiss my mother at home, let alone in public.

Mother: The mother is more responsive to the emotional and physical needs of the children. The mother also serves as the mediator between the father and child.

Common Issues of Asian Americans in America

1. **Conflict between two different cultures:** Children assimilate more rapidly than their parents. The parents reflect a traditional way of life while the children embrace the American culture for the most part.

2. **Identity Issues:** Many children born in the U.S. or who immigrated at a young age will face an identity dilemma. The issue of "Am I an American or Korean?" categorizes many children trying to understand their ethnic heritage while living in America.

3. **Language Barriers:** The 1st generation are foreign born so English would be their 2nd language. The language primarily spoken in the families by the parents are in native language while the children speak mostly English.

4. **Other Issues:** Academics, family business, interracial dating, and religion.

Family Dynamics of the KM Pastor

Family Dynamics of the EM Pastor

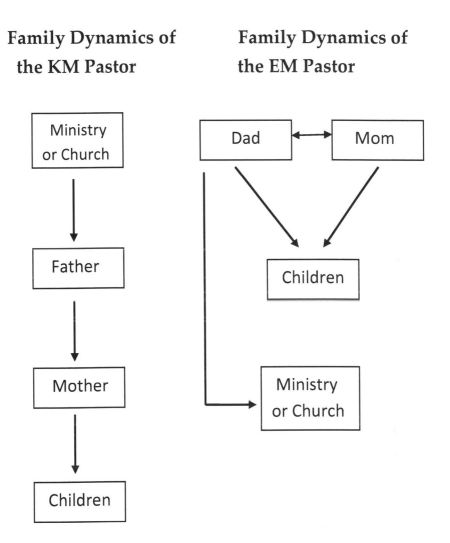

Here we see the Asian family structure in KM pastor's home vs. the EM pastor's. There is clearly a difference in priorities. If there is to be an understanding, working relationship between the 1st gen pastor and the 2nd gen pastor, it must begin with the acceptance of these two sometimes opposing points of view.

Chapter 23

Effective Leadership Unity in a Bicultural Church

Can two cultures work in unity?

One of the primary causes of tension between the 1st gen church leaders and EM pastors is different ministry philosophies. If two bicultural congregations are to succeed in one facility, then the EM pastor must realize that he needs to be under the Head Church authority.

Christian counselors will confirm that marriages fail because couples constantly try to change one another. Young couples, who doubted their compatibility before marriage, thought that they could change their spouse once they got married. Divorce results when they finally realize that they can't. Marriage itself cannot change the lifestyle and behavior patterns embedded in the person's life since childhood. Couple that with the sinful nature and we have a recipe for cemented character which only the Holy Spirit can penetrate.

The Hiring Church leaders and pastors as described by the "Traditional Asian Family Dynamics" have come from the lifestyle of behaviors, thoughts, and events of a high achievement-oriented society. These learned traditions and behaviors cannot be changed easily just because they live in America. Though the church leaders may adapt to the living environment in the U.S., the 1st gen church still operates under the traditions of the native culture. EM pastors attempted to change the ministry philosophy and programs of the immigrant church to match that of their American counterpart. And much like my personal experience with trying to change my wife, the effort bears no fruit. A good deal of complaining and trying to change something that only God can change is causing disunity.

This tension of different ministry philosophies can be reduced before the EM pastor even begins his ministry. If the EM pastor is called to the 1st gen AsiAm church, then the final question that should be answered is, "Am I willing to submit to the authority of the Head Church?" If the answer is no, then you will need to consider starting your own ministry at another church or plant a church with your particular ministry philosophy.

Unity in an Asian Church

If the answer is a solid "Yes," then even before the new candidate is hired, the bicultural ministry is considered a success. Unity in most immigrant churches is not about coming together in agreement, it is about following the rules and context of the culture in which it stands. Fighting against the culture will only lead to frustration and conflict and leave the EM pastor with a bad taste in his mouth when it comes to dealing with 1st gen leadership.

One of the roles of the EM pastor is maintaining unity between the 1st gen members and their children, the EM congregation. He reduces the "cultural gap" by becoming the "bridge builder" between the two cultures. He instinctively intercedes for both sides. While the EM the pastor gives the 2nd gen perspective about their parents, with the KM he explains what their children are thinking.

The KM thinks this way too. One EM pastor said he was asked by the 1st gen church to discipline their kids so they wouldn't be playful while learning about Christ and while at church. He boldly told the immigrant church leaders that he was there to teach the important message of Jesus and not to discipline the children. He explained that it was the parents' job to discipline and not the pastor's. This pastor was not in agreement with his leaders and soon left the church.

A popular, national, South Korean ministry called "Father's School" launched in the U.S in English with tremendous success. This ministry has now spread from coast to coast, transforming many traditional Asian households to Christ centered ones. The Duranno Father School was developed in South Korea as an evangelical response to concerns over uninvolved Korean fathers. The program which was founded in 1995 confronts men's irresponsibility to lead the family and promotes involvement and positive fathering. The article from KoreAm cites Hyun Kyu In, director of USA Fathers School in Los Angeles, *"The father's influence cannot be understated. Men must show their love in front of their children, to touch and even kiss their wives publicly, to be reconciled with their own fathers. All of these things translate to the likelihood of better relations with their own children."*[19] With small group activities, testimonials, lectures, and teaching on how to write love letters to children and wives, the "Father's School" ministry is changing the views of Korean men from the traditional way of relating to their families to the biblical way.

The 1st gen church leaders need to accept that though the EM pastors might not understand their native background and language, they do understand love.

The Language might be a barrier
The Culture might be a barrier
But there is NO barrier to love

Missionaries are taught from the beginning that even though the culture and the language of the people they are reaching are different, the non-believers understand the significance of care and affection. Though the EM pastors might not understand fully what is being said, they will recognize the effort, care, and encouragement the Head Church leaders are putting into the relationship. Ultimately, it will be the efforts of the leaders that will conquer the barriers of culture and language that separate the second gen leaders from the first.

> If the EM pastor is called to the immigrant church, then the final question that must be considered is, "Am I willing to submit to the authority of the head church?"

Relationship Overview

Relationship differences in a bicultural context are best described by Rev. Victor Lee:

> *Relationships in the Chinese culture tend to be quite structured, stemming from the family and extending to the general society. Chinese families have been traditionally hierarchical in nature. The husband is the head of the home*

where most decisions are made. Positionally, he is like a monarch who rules the entire clan, and whatever he decides is seldom changed. With ascription and harmony being highly valued, obedience becomes a predominant characteristic of the Chinese culture and obedience is thus, a demonstration of respect (where obedience is often equated with spirituality). No one dares to openly challenge the decision of the head in this authoritatively based system, including the wife. Challenges and objections disrupt this harmony and openly show disrespect to the head. The same holds true in the workplace and in society. The older the person the more respect and obedience is given. There is much pressure in this environment to conform to the way things have always been done and to maintain the status quo. Change and conflict are usually internalized, unspoken or overlooked. Any form of disagreement is usually very threatening to the head of the house, employer, or elder. It is seldom dealt with in public but when surfaced, the head always has the last say. [20]

Lee nails it when he states, *"Challenges and objections disrupt this harmony and openly show disrespect to the head."* Keeping the harmony from a traditional perspective is keeping the unity. And in order for unity to exist, there must be submission to authority. It is difficult for a 2nd gen EM pastor who has grown up in a culture of group oriented management with lively discussions and disagreements to have a submissive role in a traditional hierarchal compliance system. However, if the EM pastor is willing to submit to the authority of the traditional Asian leadership of the church, then ministry unity and success will follow.

Rev. Lee gives an overview of the differences and challenges faced by the 1st and 2nd generations:

Basis for Decision

1st Generation: Direction from authority

2nd Generation: Discussion, agreement/disagreement

Forms of Control

1st Generation: Compliance to rules/laws, with rewards/punishment

2nd Generation: Interpersonal consensus and group commitments

Position to Others

1st Generation: Hierarchical

2nd Generation: Peer

Relationally

1st Generation: Structured and formal

2nd Generation: Group-oriented

To be Avoided

1st Generation: Deviation from authority

2nd Generation: Failure to reach consensus

Can you imagine what it would be like if Timothy disagreed with Apostle Paul? What if Timothy said something like, "Apostle Paul, I don't mean to down play the 1st gen Christian mind set of running a church, but I don't think you understand that now there are better approaches to church leadership for today's complex church issues. I just came back from the 'Innovative Church Leadership Conference' held in the modern city of Rome, and I learned so much about making church relevant to our community."

What if Joshua said to Moses? "Thank you Moses. It's about time you asked me to take over. I watched you lead the people out of Egypt and adjudicate their disputes, but I've been schooled at the 'Innovative Church Leadership Conference' and heard Andy Stanley, John Maxwell (I've read all his leadership books), Dave Gibbons, Frances Chan, and many others talk about having a powerful vision to empower our people to reach the next level of effectiveness for God's kingdom. I'm sorry, but your old ministry philosophy is not going to work on the 2nd and 3rd generation Israelites."

> However, if the EM pastor is willing to submit to the authority of the traditional Asian leadership of the church, then ministry unity and success will follow.

We know that Timothy and Joshua did not assert themselves this way. In fact they carried the traditions of their leaders to the next generation. How ironic it is that there are so many "new" church programs, materials, resources, methods, and leadership training and development seminars, and yet the examples of successful ministry lie in the Scriptures right before our eyes. Success begins with submission.

> Keeping the harmony from a traditional perspective is keeping the unity. And in order for unity to exist, one side must be willing to submit to the authority for a culture of harmony to play its role.

Submission to Authority is God's command

If the EM pastor is called to fully submit to the authority of the 1st immigrant Head church leadership because he is called there, God will prosper the church. The greatest benefit the EM pastor will receive by this act of submission is spiritual maturity. Submission does not necessarily mean obedience, but it is an attitude of respect for the authority God has placed over him. If for nothing else, the EM pastor should be giving respect to the 1st gen leadership because of their relative age. But to honor them with his cooperation and service would show that he can be a Timothy to a Paul. Godly men were entrusted with authority over others for the purpose of leading them: *"Obey your leaders and submit to their authority. They keep watch over you as men who must give an account. Obey them so that their work will be a joy, not a burden, for that would be of no advantage to you"* (Hebrews 13:17).

When I started working for a church, my wife had to remind me constantly that I was not working for the Head church and its leaders, but for the Lord. And the Lord commands me to submit to my church authorities. He placed people in authority over me to guide me, as Paul reminds us that *"everyone must submit himself to the governing authorities" (Ro. 13:1).* And we will answer to God if we do not submit to authority. *"So then, each of us will give an account of himself to God" (Ro. 14:12).*

Romans 13:1, 5

¹Everyone must submit himself to the governing authorities, for there is no authority except that which God has established. The authorities that exist have been established by God.

⁵Therefore, it is necessary to submit to the authorities, not only because of possible punishment but also because of conscience.

The Scripture is clear that authority has been established by God. Therefore those under authority should submit to the governing body assigned to them. The authorities are set up to ensure that those under it will do what is good and right and recognize the order of hierarchy for decision making. The Head church leaders oversee the EM pastors; however, each person must give an account to God for his actions.

Exodus 23:20-21

²⁰ *"See, I am sending an angel ahead of you to guard you along the way and to bring you to the place I have prepared. ²¹ Pay attention to him and listen to what he says. Do not rebel against him; he will not forgive your rebellion, since my Name is in him.*

Chapter 24

Interview with EM Pastor John Tung

Leadership in the Asian American Church

Interviewee: EM pastor John Tung
Interviewer: Joseph Choi
Name of church: Chinese Bible Church of Maryland (CBCM)

Joseph: Pastor John, how long have you been a pastor?

John: Pastor for 24 years in all. I have been the English pastor of CBCM for 20 years.

Joseph: What is the size and make-up of your church?

John: 1000 people, including kids. Make-up: About 92% Chinese, 8% non-Chinese. Worship services in 3 languages: Cantonese, English, and Mandarin. We have Chinese from many different countries of origin and who can speak many languages or dialects besides English and Chinese. We have a (tri lingual) senior pastor, a Cantonese pastor, an English pastor and a youth pastor. We are also looking for a young adults pastor.

Joseph: How did you get started as a pastor?

John: I felt called when I started seminary. I was going to seminary for some general theological training, and after the first year, felt God nudging me to keep going forward. I went into ministry because of a calling that I could help the Chinese church and also because of the need I saw for English-speaking pastors in the Chinese church.

Joseph: How did you end up at this church?

John: My wife and I were open to some other ministry after four years in our first ministry, and we met the Senior Pastor of the current church I am serving and they were searching for an English Pastor and God seemed to be bringing us together to find a new stage of ministry for them and me.

Joseph: What were the most important criteria for you in choosing this church?

John: Theologically, I could agree with its statement of faith. We liked its vision and direction. We also liked it because it was in an area with a large Chinese population and people our age.

Joseph: What is a highlight in working for this church?

John: The great warmth of the people here. They (the lay people) are also very active in serving. I feel there are many coworkers and servants in the church – each doing what he can to contribute to the overall outreach and ministry.

Joseph: What was the worst time while working for your church?

John: When some active people began to leave our church over issues concerning the direction of our church's ministry.

Joseph: What was the leadership like for the FiGI Chinese Church? Was your church leadership different than other 1st gen Chinese churches?

John: Our church is unusual for an immigrant church because when our church started 34 years ago, it was already more Americanized due to more people who had grown up in the U.S. Our board meetings and staff meetings have ALWAYS been held ONLY in English. We had some ABC (American-born Chinese) elders when the church began. The church saw the equality of ministries in English and Mandarin and Cantonese from early on. And the church had adults who were from all three groups. Plus there were numerous intermarriages between ABCs and (Overseas-born Chinese) OBCs in its history. This church has had a sense of its "bicultural" and "bi-lingual" tendencies from early on. The Senior Pastor can also preach in all 3 languages. I can speak Mandarin and English. Many of our leaders can speak more than 1 language fluently and have been in the US many years. But there was a strong sense that we need to stay together to maximize our ministry capabilities and outreach potential, trying to find ways to meet each language and cultural group's specific needs, but also finding ways to pool resources and work together. Many Chinese families have spouses who prefer one language to another, kids who speak English and grandparents who like their own native language or dialect. So, we felt a church needed to be able to meet all these kinds of needs under one roof.

Joseph: What was the turning point of your leadership?

John: When I realized that I had to take more leadership for the English-speaking adults and preach better and outreach more and develop more ministries for English-speakers.

Joseph: Did you ever consider changing your leadership style, direction, vision, or mission of your congregation? Did you have a vision for your ministry when you first began or did you just go with the flow?

John: Yes, I've had to reinvent myself 3-4 times in the 20 years here. I had to keep growing and staying sharp, otherwise our ministry would have become stale and lost energy. I learned that the key to ministry is a growing minister. I also have tried to work with other staff members and realized that we need one another and we each have our own specialty.

Joseph: What is your vision for the church in the future?

John: Keep discerning what God is doing in our midst and how to respond to those divine workings. We also have more people who are reaching middle age or older so we need to find some ways to motivate them to serve in their "second-half." I am also trying to find ways to have the different ages of English speakers (teens to adults) to share resources and contribute their strengths. I think as we become even more a part of America, we also have a challenge of impacting and serving Montgomery County and our local areas.

Joseph: If you were to retire, how do you plan to have the successor fill your role?

John: Good question. I haven't thought too much of that yet.

Joseph: What are the commonalities of 1st immigrant Chinese American churches across United States? Are there normal issues facing the majority of them in regards to the EM pastor relations?

John: We are two cultures or more. So, the ability to cross these cultural gaps and work together is one of the keys. There is also the vital need for theological agreement in order to keep working together. The issue of the relationship between the Chinese-speaking leadership and English-speaking leadership is very important, which affects the relationship between the Senior Pastor and Associate Pastor (or EM). The more they have in common and the more they shared in culture, the better it is. This doesn't mean they have to be the same, but a high degree of respect and seeing the importance of both ministry, the more likely the possibility of success and good working relationship.

Joseph: What are your recommendations in regard to having a successful EM and head church relationship? What are the criteria in looking for one?

John: The ability to be BRIDGES to one another. The Asian church is a bicultural and bilingual church – you just cannot escape this fact. High ability to understand, (put yourself in each other's point of view), support for each other's ministry, and ... English-speaking ADULT leadership (even if only a small group) makes for a ... good ministry.

Joseph: What advice would you give to the head church looking for an EM pastor?

John: Have a senior pastor who can work with the EM (pastor). Having other English speaking lay leaders in a church to work with EM (pastor) is important. Having the ability to forgive and understand the EM (pastor). Give the EM (pastor) plenty of encouragement. It can feel very lonely at times as an EM (pastor) in the immigrant church. Support the EM (pastor's) family and make sure they have people like themselves for support and fellowship. The EM (pastor) is not only a servant, but also needs to be served.

Joseph: What advice would you give to an EM pastor looking to work for an Asian Church?

John: I regard perseverance, longevity (since also Asians value and respect age and experience) in one church to be key ingredients. Seminaries don't teach you how to work in an immigrant church – it's more "caught" than "taught." Learning to use your personal strengths, the strengths of your culture, and the strengths of the American church are essential foundations in working for an Asian church.

[Interview with EM Pastor John Tung[21]]

Questions to Answer:

1. Are you called to be an EM pastor? (Determining the ministry context is essential before embarking on the journey)

_____

_____

_____

_____

_____

_____

2. Are you called to this specific church/ministry?

_____

_____

_____

_____

_____

3. What is the purpose that God has given you for this specific church/ministry?

_____

_____

_____

_____

_____

4. Are you willing to follow God's purpose for that church/ministry?

_____

_____

_____

_____

_____

5. Are you willing to submit yourself to the governing authorities that God has assigned to you in that specific church/ministry?

_____

_____

_____

_____

_____

6. Are you willing to persevere, resolve, and reconcile through potential conflicts?

_____

_____

_____

_____

_____

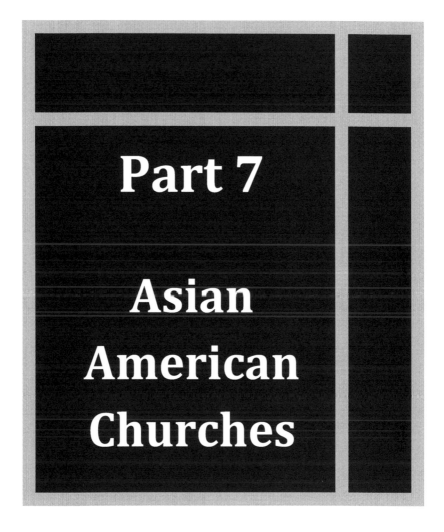

Part 7

Asian American Churches

E very 1st gen KM pastor who plants a church anticipates hiring an EM pastor as his church grows. This is a common practice in almost all 1st gen Korean and Chinese churches because the need of the 2nd generation children. Hiring an EM/Youth pastor is inevitable if the church is to keep the growing number of 2nd generation members from departing their parents' church.

7

Asian American Churches

Pastor Kim, a first gen Korean pastor, was looking into a local area to plant a church. One item on his checklist was to be near a seminary. Pastor Kim understood the dynamics of planting a Korean-American church, and the advantage of being near a seminary meant the church would have a major source of ministry leaders. A Korean church in the Midwest planted their ministry within a mile of a large Bible college because they knew that the turnover rate was high among EM and youth pastors. It would be unheard of but if a senior pastor does not anticipate hiring an EM pastor, he will be caught off guard because the congregation will demand it. It must be included in the plans of the church plant.

What should be the Head church's ultimate vision for an EM congregation? What should the EM strive for? Should the EM work toward becoming an "independent church model," a "duplex," or a "multi-ethnic church"? Is an independent EM truly independent?

In 2005 a new EM pastor began working at a church with 200 plus members. Collegians, professionals, married couples, families and even EM deacons were already established. The EM was classified as "independent" which meant that the EM had autonomy to oversee its own operations. The new EM pastor had an agreement with the senior KM pastor to have EM become a separate identity as a church plant in the future. The agreement was to grow the English Ministry in a five to seven year period before moving out of the facility they were sharing. However, five years later a new senior KM pastor came on board and requested the EM to come under the leadership of the KM. Understandably, this midstream course correction disturbed the EM pastor because the original agreement was to establish a second gen church plant, and returning to be under the leadership of the KM would mean that full autonomy would be lost. Subsequently, the EM pastor departed with 20 % of the EM congregation.

Was the EM truly "independent" when the new EM pastor came on board? The EM cannot be classified as "independent" when the head church is still paying for EM's rent, church operation expenses, and the pastor's paycheck. In many Asian churches there is still confusion concerning the exact classification of the EM ministry. This section will delineate the general stages of Asian churches and their classifications.

Church Plant Story

A Lay Leader

We got married in the 80s and as soon as we got married, my in-laws suggested (strongly) that since we were now adults, we should consider attending a Korean church, as if that was somehow the proper rite of passage into adulthood. Prior to getting married, neither one of us had any desire to worship, less serve at a Korean church. In my immature mind, I vowed that I would stay far away from Korean churches. Prior to my marriage, I was last attending a large conservative spiritually dry Presbyterian Church. Honestly, this church was not doing much for my spiritual growth. But my justification for attending this church was that I was at least keeping the Sabbath. Meanwhile, my new bride was attending a vibrant cutting edge charismatic church in another region. Unlike me, she was blessed to be part of a vibrant and dynamic church where she was spiritually nurtured. But going back to our parent's "suggestion," the burden of filial piety indoctrinated into our Korean psyche since birth made us capitulate without resistance.

So we started to attend a well established Korean immigrant church with around 300 attendees. No sooner than when our rears warmed up the wooden pews, we were asked by one of the deacons to teach Sunday school for college kids. I felt honored, but I knew they had the wrong guy, because I may have grown up in church all my life, even as a third generation Christian, but I was not a teacher by any stretch, and I had never taught or led so much as a small group Bible study. They did not ask for my resume, nor did they conduct a background check. By association, because my wife was the daughter and I was the son-in-law of a respected deacon and deaconess, we automatically qualified. And the added bonus was that we spoke

English. I certainly did not have any confidence in taking on this role, but I trusted that my wife was well versed in the Word, so quietly leaning on her Biblical acumen; I/we agreed to serve.

The following Sunday, without any instructions or guidance whatsoever, we were given the church choir closet, an 8' x 12' room, equipped with nothing but a single small window, furnished with a rack with choir robes, a folding desk and chairs, and of course, 2 college-age kids to teach. My assumption is that these poor kids were forcibly thrown into our care. With no other directive other than to teach these kids about God (we assumed), we decided to have fun. Because we experienced so much boredom and lack of connectivity while growing up in Korean churches, we knew that a practically irrelevant and boring study and reflection of the Word was only going to turn these kids away from church.

Over the ensuing months, we simply shared about our lives and our walk with God, as the spirit led. For the students who were no more than 5-6 years younger than us, I believe it was both strange and yet "cool" to spend time with English speaking Koreans, who could not only relate through language, but understood their cultural dualism and dilemmas.

The combination of our chemistry as a couple teaching team, and our homegrown but clueless approach to Sunday school was working, by God's grace. The kids kept coming back week after week, slowly bringing along their friends. Word also got around and more parents began sending them to our class. Additionally, the senior pastor who took the helm of the church, just before we arrived was an anointed teacher. Thus, the church was experiencing steady growth. In less than a year, we were so packed in the choir closet that we had to be moved out of that space. The crowding was not the real problem. We were having so much fun doing Sunday school that we got really loud at times. The clincher was that the choir dressing room was right behind the pulpit. So while the adults were having a holy and consecrated time in the sanctuary, we were having a Bible frat party in the room. We had deacons occasionally pop in the room to shush us, as we tried to control ourselves.

But even as the Sunday school ministry grew to the point where two dozen college students descended upon the class, the church's feeble attempt at an English service was barely staying afloat. As with most Korean American immigrant churches, the English service was by and large a glorified babysitting service to keep the kids in church and the family unit intact in one church. Somewhere along our journey, this sad state of affairs was brought to our attention by the senior pastor. He asked us to help. We agreed to do so, provided we could do whatever we needed to, to breathe life into the EM service.

The one thing we knew that we absolutely had to incorporate into this English service was a vibrant and spirit-filled worship. My wife and I each had the privilege of experiencing this type of worship environment while involved in our previous churches and school-based Christian fellowships. Worship was a passion for us, as anointed worship was foundational in both of our spiritual lives. We really wanted to share this blessing with our Korean believers. Hence, we rounded up a few kids who could play instruments, which was not too difficult in a Korean church, and starting with a guitar and a piano, and gradually built up a worship team. The ministry began to take shape and bear good fruits. It got to the point where we needed to invest in some instruments and equipment so we dug into our pockets and equipped a full praise and worship band.

Despite our total lack of experience in ministry, and the many mistakes we made along the way, the meager investment we gave to the Lord eventually bore fruit. The English service steadily grew *from a dozen to eventually around seventy-eighty by the fifth year. Somewhere along this journey, an associate pastor was officially assigned to preach at the English services. But even while the growth of the English service was acknowledged by the church leadership by this appointment of a "real" pastor instead of a lay minister, the church leaders did not look too kindly at the yards of connecting wires, speakers, instruments, and most of all, the dreaded drum set. We had to have the team dismantle and remove the equipment from the pulpit area quickly before the Korean service started, in order to avoid the disapproving look of some of the conservative leaders. The sense I got was that in their opinion, we were just kids messing around in church. It was that frustration and feeling that our effort and passion for church was not being accepted, that made us jump at our next ministry opportunity.*

Half a decade after we had inadvertently stumbled into ministry, we found out that our senior pastor was getting ready to move on and leave our church to plant a new church in a totally different part of the country. In many ways, as he was exposed to non-Korean and non-traditional churches in his training and personal walk in Christ, I believe that he was also frustrated by the limitations set for him by the leadership and institution of the traditional Korean church. This young pastor was a rare commodity back then, as he could preach perfectly in Korean, while also being able to do a great job in English. On top of that, he was an anointed preacher. Although he was born and raised in Korea, most of his young adulthood was spent in the U.S. including his college and seminary years. Sensing his frustration with the church, and harboring an empathetic passion in our hearts to minister to folks that God had sent our way over the previous years, we decided to seize the moment.

We invited our pastor and his wife to dinner and shared our vision for a new kind of Korean church where the floundering and slowly dissipating 1 and 1.5 generation Korean Americans can worship in a culturally relevant environment, in a language that could touch their hearts, and where worship was vibrant, dynamic, open and where they could experience the move of the Holy Spirit with power and freedom. We made a case for starting this new church experiment right here in our city, and asked him to seriously consider this proposition, assuring him of our commitment for ministry partnership and support in this venture, especially with regard to the English service. After several days of prayer, our pastor called to let us know that we are going for it! He resigned as soon as he made his decision.

The rest became history as we launched a new church plant several months later with a team of half a dozen families. It was a very successful launch. After half a year of praying and preparing at our house the church burst out of the gate running. The inaugural service was attended by over 300 people, and month after month, it just kept growing. It broke a thousand attendees in the first three-four years.

By most standards this was huge a success. However, the English service, which we had envisioned to be the lead purpose for which this church was launched, steadily took a back seat as the Korean services continued to grow exponentially while the English service grew merely by addition. There was not much that we could do to prevent this from happening as the tide of the times flowed favorably towards a rapid growth in the Korean service. That is where the numbers were. That is where the tithes and offerings flowed, and ergo, the economic driver of the church. The English service comprised of mostly high school and college students and a handful of young professionals just starting out on their careers. As a group, the passions of the English-speaking congregation far outpaced its lackluster economic prowess and ability to contribute significantly to the organizational structure of the church, at many levels.

Gradually our senior pastor's efforts and eventually, even the passion was pulled toward the Korean services. Even the makeup of the church leadership started to assume the shape and character of a traditional Korean-American immigrant church in its organizational structure and spirit. While the church continued to be successful by most standards, some aspects of the original reason for the church plant were maintained and uncompromised, including the spiritual fruitfulness and the style of worship. In our minds, the primary goal for which we had invested into this ministry had virtually stalled.

By all means, the English service was not terminated, nor deliberately ignored by the leadership, but it did not receive the priority attention or the resources and investment it needed to become the primary mission objective of this church. Unfortunately, in hindsight, we did not have the leadership experience or a real understanding of the situation.

Without a strategy to correct the course and sensing a spiritual desert ahead for the unfulfilled passions in our souls, we quietly left the church after five years of labor of love, and never really looked back. Since then, even though God continued to keep our passion lit for the next generation Korean-American churches, we never returned to do ministry in a purely Korean church context.

Chapter 25

Asian American Church Models

What is your current church model?

The Family Model

Since the cultural emphasis in Asian communities is the family, it is natural for AsiAm churches to operate in a manner similar to what happens in the home. The family model or sometimes called the "paternal model" or "house model" is where the church operates similar to the traditional Asian family where leadership is not shared but ranked through a hierarchical system. The majority of the AsiAm churches are planted with a single family style structure. It is typical in this stage for a pastor or lay leader to find any volunteer who can speak English to help serve the English speaking members. The majority of the EM members in this stage are children and youth. Eventually as the EM congregation grows, it will seek its own identity and will search for a leader to primarily work with this group. As seen in the "Church Plant Story," someone saw a need and looked for people who spoke English. Under this model the EM is covered and budgeted by the Head church and operates as part of the overall KM ministry without an independent name or budget. The EM is dependent upon the KM to operate its ministry and supply a leader who speaks English.

The Self-rule Model

The Self-rule model or sometimes called an "independent" or "autonomous" model is the second stage of the EM journey. As the EM becomes more self-sufficient with its own leaders governing and overseeing the EM congregation, the KM pretty much lets them run the ministry. This frees up the KM to focus on its own ministry. The EM may even establish its own non-profit name and provide for its own budget, but this is all done based on the agreement between the KM and the EM. Most of the churches in this particular model are not fully "independent" from the Head church. The classification of the word "independent" would not be suitable for this stage since the Head Church still pays for the general expense of the facility and other operations costs.

Example of Self-rule Model
(Changes been made for anonymity)

Eventually the Lord called Pastor Yang to leave First Baptist Church and plant a church in Alabama. In December of 1994, Pastor Yang became the new head pastor for the English Ministry. Coincidentally, this was also the time that we witnessed an explosive growth in the number of married couples in the church. As to be expected these married couples were transforming themselves into families. The Lord has blessed this congregation with an abundance of children that necessitated the creation of the children's ministry.

Not only did the demographics change, the English Ministry also was reorganized; consisting of college students, young single adults and married couples and families.

As the members of the church grew older, they became better equipped to handle more of the responsibilities of governing church affairs. Eventually, the Session (Korean Ministry Board of Elders) recognized the English Ministry's ability to oversee its own operations and granted them functional autonomy. During this time we confirmed our first deacons and soon after a diaconal board... Pastor Yang envisioned an autonomous second-generation church, with its own elders, partnering with the first generation congregation...

The Duplex Model

The "duplex" model is sometimes called the "partnership" or "bicultural" model, the concept that there are two churches under one roof. The EM has full autonomy in the day to day operations and budget. The EM leaders have the freedom to custom design their own ministry in achieving their distinct vision, mission, and core values. Some "duplex" model churches will work cohesively with the 1st gen church, creating an inter-dependent ministry. The EM structure and policies are in complete control of the EM leadership. However, there are some limitations if the EM is using the same facility with the Head Church. Typically, the dominant group is the KM, and their schedule comes first when using the building. Even if the prime time slot is given to the EM, the probability of adding a second EM session is difficult. Furthermore, in most of the "Duplex" model cases, the head church still pays for the mortgage and other operational expenses albeit some of those may be paid for by the EM. When the Head Church pays for the operations costs of the facility, ultimately they will have the last say.

Independent / Church Plant Model

In this model the EM church "identity" has been freed from the Head Church. The new "Independent" church plant has its own covenant, policy, and rule including all operations and facility costs. The former "EM" leaders are now in complete control. There is absolutely no reporting to the KM. The "Church Plant" or "Independent Church Plant" occurs when the EM has left the facility of the 1st gen church and plants a new church. One primary issue facing the leaders of this new church plant is defining who they are. When the English congregation was connected to the Head Church, it had an identity as an EM, but by becoming a church plant, it lost that identity, thus the need for a new one.

A Lay Leader's Story:
(Changes been made for anonymity)

A Lay Leader writes:

Second Bible Church is a non-denominational church in the Detroit area. Second Bible Church is a small church around hundred members with most of the members being 1.5 generation Korean

Americans. *The demographics are middle to upper middle class young professionals with children.*

Second Bible Church is in its eleventh year in existence since its separation from the Korean Church, a predominantly first-generation Korean congregation. A key motivation for the separation was a desire to become a multi-ethnic church. While as part of the English Ministry (EM) at Second Bible Church, there was (a) large percentage of non-Koreans. This prompted the EM leaders to focus their efforts on multi-ethnicity and felt that while they were still under the roof and ministry of a Korean church they were somewhat stifled.

What started off with high hopes in the beginning became somewhat diminished over the years when reality set upon a young and inexperienced church. The reality is that just because you want to become a multi-ethnic church doesn't mean that is what you are. The fact is Second Bible Church is a niche church that caters toward 1.5 generation Koreans. Although there were many non-Koreans that came through the doors, most or all did not stay long. Not that we didn't try, as a matter of fact, sometimes we tried too hard. Focusing all our energy to make sure they felt right at home; however, over time they left for various reasons.

Second Bible Church has since given up hope of becoming a multi-ethnic church and focused more on being a niche church to 1.5 generation Korean-Americans. We've gone through some changes over the years where many of the core leaders left the church during one tumultuous year right before the senior pastor decided to move onto a new phase in his career. Now the church was in the process of finding our new senior pastor position. Some of the important things we were looking for in a new senior pastor candidate were:

1. *Can he preach? After-all, his key role will be to preach from the Bible effectively.*
2. *Seminary graduate*
3. *His direction for the future of the church – vision*
4. *Asian (Korean preferred)? Second Bible Church was a predominantly Asian church*
5. *Personality...will he be able to get along?*
6. *Whole package – how is his spouse? Will she be able to get along with other wives and women in the church?*

Now with a new senior pastor for over three years and new leadership at the helm, the church has grown to its current size around one hundred members and stabilized. Although stabilization is a nice change from no member leaving through the back doors each month, we are ready for some growth. Unfortunately, our church has not only become a niche church for 1.5 generation Korean-Americans but 1.5 generation couples with young children which has limited our outreach potential and growth. The few young singles – youth, college students, and single professionals (that) have come through the doors...ceased to show up the following Sundays after seeing the limited number of members in their social makeup. This has been an area of concern for the leadership...

Within the last year, the church has looked at one additional significant change – joining a denomination. This can have a huge change on the makeup and look of the church. Although Second Bible Church has always prided itself as being an independent church (no affiliation with a church or a denomination), the leadership team feels that this is a move that is necessary. Without going into too much detail, we feel this will help in multiple areas:

- *Training and support for the pastoral staff and leadership*
- *Collaborated efforts in mission's work*
- *Pastoral search assistance*
- *Opportunities to join in community outreach*
- *Attend joint activities (i.e. VBS, retreats, etc)*

Although this church has not officially made the decision to join the denomination… (it) looks like the move is imminent. Personally I am looking forward to the change and being part of this denomination so that ultimately Jesus can be glorified. After all, that is why a church exists.

Chapter 26

Authors' Final Thoughts

Reflection/Belief/Opinion/Philosophy

Thoughts on Asian Church Models

Not many independent church plants by EM pastors survive long when the EM congregation has branched out of the KM as a result of conflicts. Statistics prove that those who go into a second marriage will have a higher risk of divorce because the first marital issues were never resolved. Church plants from conflicts have a tendency to fail if reconciliation and forgiveness is not a priority. When conflicts arise at the new church plant, the leaders or the members might run just like they did when they were with the KM. The successful church plants are those that have been blessed by the KM to be fully independent. They become the independent church plants that both the KM and EM have been pursuing and praying for. Even after the plant the relationship with the sending church remains very much respectful.

The successful independent church plants reach around 100 to 150 congregation members on average over a five to ten year period. Some receive financial and resource support for a few years until it can operate fully on its own. But if the church plant begins with less than 50 adult members, the church usually fails. EM members are not used to giving like their parents who have faithfully invested in their church. On the other hand if the EM members are committed to the new church and understand that finances are an issue, they will give sacrificially in order to maintain their independent status. The pastor will need to speak frankly about their financial situation so that the congregation is compelled to respond.

If the desire of the EM is to be an "independent church plant," then the leadership of both the EM and KM should take some time to pray about this serious matter and do some research in order to make an informed decision. The first question to ask God would be, "Is it your will for us to become an independent church plant?" Churches may be planted based on congregation size, finances, vision, and potential, but they don't survive if it was never in the Lord's will or it wasn't the right timing. When leaders pray, God responds by planting purpose and passion in their hearts, so God's purpose in planting the church bears fruit. Human ingenuity will only lead to frustration because He opposes the proud. Without His purpose in the hearts of the leaders, a strategy of growth will only be by human means. What must God do for those who want to plant an independent church? So much more than they realize. Many church plants that failed testify to this truth. There are two primary purposes of prayer:

1. The supreme purpose of prayer is to honor and glorify God.
2. Prayer is requesting God to manifest His goodness and glory in people's lives.

In the book _New Beginning: I've accepted Christ – now what?_ The authors wrote, "_Praying to Almighty God is an opportunity to magnify Him so come into His presence recognizing who God is and what He can do for you._"[22]

When considering a church plant, we must ask the question, "Are we magnifying God in what we are doing? And, will this church plant honor and glorify Him?" Paul warns:

Galatians 3:3
Are you so foolish? After beginning with the Spirit, are you now trying to attain your goal by human effort?

Prayer is an opportunity to receive clarity, insight, and confirmation to plant a church. If you feel like you're having a hard time hearing from God, then try the "Pray and Listen" approach, along with journaling, to clearly hear from God. The procedure is very simple. Make a commitment for 30 days to pray for 30 minutes and listen to the Lord for 30 minutes. As you listen have your journal ready and write down everything that is going through your mind. Some will be relevant and some will not be, but God will give you perspective you've never had. He will bring to mind things you've never thought of that need to be considered. Ask the Lord for Scriptural insight so you can learn from what He has said.

Once the calling to plant a church is confirmed, the second step is to draw up a one-year budget for the new church plant. Overestimate everything in the budget so there is a cushion for unexpected expenses. The final stage of preparation would be to role play the meetings, operations, programs, activities, and any other aspects of a church plant to see how everything would flow. Since many church plants run an evangelism program to reach out to their community, it would be important for potential church planters to research and practice through a good evangelism plan.

It is vital to have an idea of the potential number of people that will be your core team. And rating your core team members' participation from low to high will give you the proper strategy in assigning their roles and responsibilities in the beginning of the church plant. Trying to mobilize a team at the last minute will lead to unnecessary and avoidable frustration. No company releases a product into the market without first testing it on a small group. The stress of planting a church can be dramatically reduced if it is well-planned and role played.

Proverbs 16:3
[3] *Commit to the LORD whatever you do,*
and he will establish your plans.

What model does the Head Church ultimately desire for the EM? What model does the EM congregation desire to become?

If the EM website does not have the answers to these questions, ask them during the interview. The majority of the immigrant churches have never considered what church model they desire for the EM and a good deal of the 1st gen pastors have never asked the EM what final model they would like to pursue. Unless the EM is a completely independent church plant, the Head Church should make the final decision in the direction of the EM. Answering these questions will help the Head Church leaders and the hiring committee probe deeper into their thoughts concerning their future destination. This will help the new candidate decide if the direction of the Head Church for the EM is in alignment with his views, then formulating a vision and implementing the strategies and goals will be much easier.

If you're going on a road trip and you know where you want to go, it's much easier if you map out a course to your destination.

The road map can guide you and help you choose the best route. Having a clear picture of the church model can guide the EM toward their unique "identity." If the Head Church and the EM congregation have similar images of their destination, then the new candidate will have a greater chance of success building toward it.

Thoughts on Leadership

During the growing stage of my business, I used to call every one of my clients to wish them "Happy Thanksgiving" the day before Thanksgiving. When the number of clients reached 150, I still called each member personally. When membership reached 200, I thought about sending cards, but realized it wasn't as personable as calling. My overarching goal for the business was to make each person feel significant and part of the family. When it reached over 300, things were getting much more challenging. It was at this turning point of my business growth that I started to do more in-depth research on leadership.

I'm still learning and developing leadership skills. At the age of eight, I was assisting my brothers in martial art classes, by age thirteen I was teaching my own class, and by sixteen I ran my own martial arts studio with my brother as the owner. At sixteen I was a full-fledged business man. I knew how to write contracts, develop marketing strategies, negotiate with clients, close sales, design curriculum, and most importantly recruit, train, and develop leaders. I took the spiritual gift assessment test once a year over the past five years and every time I did, leadership was either number one or two. Leadership development is one of my areas of passion and I'm constantly trying to learn, improve, and grow as a leader, father, and husband. However, is this what God desires for me or does He desire something much greater?

Churches should hire pastors with leadership skills, pastors who can move the congregation to achieve its vision and mission as planned by God. However, should "leadership" be the defining goal for a pastor?

In the last decade there has been a countless number of books on leadership and it may be the most emphasized topic in the business and church ministry fields. New books are being introduced faster than leaders could read them. It's an "all you can eat" leadership buffet here in the U.S. Why is that? Perhaps, it's because we live in a "fatherless" generation, and men hunger for practical steps on becoming a leader. Pressure also comes from large and mega churches marketing leadership as the key to success and church members desiring to see their churches move like the secular world. The expectation is that pastors should be "hero" leaders, capable of commanding the respect of the church and the public because they are so effective.

The statistics are clear; finding good role models in the U.S. is difficult. Even if we find one, they may disappoint us at any moment. The ones that are respected write books on leadership. But are we starting to become "copy cat" leaders in the U.S? Has our unique and special DNA created by God taken the back seat behind what everyone else desires for pastors to become? God has given each one of us a very unique DNA to accomplish His will on earth, using our strengths and our weaknesses. All the personal assessment tests, spiritual gifts inventories, and leadership development programs will do us no good if we don't know why God made us in the first place. Our uniqueness is only good if we know what it's for. If everyone was like John Maxwell, who would be Bill Hybels, and if everyone was like Bill Hybels, who would be

Billy Graham? God has given each person a special identity with skills to be used by the Holy Spirit.

Exodus 31:1-6

¹ Then the LORD said to Moses, ² "See, I have chosen Bezalel son of Uri, the son of Hur, of the tribe of Judah, ³ and I have filled him with the Spirit of God, with skill, ability and knowledge in all kinds of crafts- ⁴ to make artistic designs for work in gold, silver and bronze, ⁵ to cut and set stones, to work in wood, and to engage in all kinds of craftsmanship. ⁶ Moreover, I have appointed Oholiab son of Ahisamach, of the tribe of Dan, to help him. Also I have given skill to all the craftsmen to make everything I have commanded you:

Jae and I strongly believe in leadership, and we are passionate about it, but what we're more passionate about is being fully devoted followers of Jesus Christ. Being a Christian must come before the exercise of our own leadership ability. If you are gifted in leadership and you are in the AsiAm church, then patiently and with humility work alongside and under the 1st gen church leaders.

> God has given each person a special identity with skills to be led extraordinarily by the Holy Spirit.

Who was responsible for the explosion of church growth in the first century, and in a matter of days grew the church to over 5000? *"I planted the seed, Apollos watered it, but God made it grow. So neither he who plants nor he who waters is anything, but only God, who makes things grow"* (1 Cor. 3:6-7). Everyone knows that it was God who added 3,000 members on the Day of Pentecost (Acts 2:41). How would you like to start a church with 3,000 members? And it didn't even stop there because the *"Lord added to their number daily those who were being saved" (Acts 2:47).*

So what is the bottom line in becoming an effective leader? Prayer! Dave Earley noted, *"The difference between mild stirrings and deep breakthroughs is prayer. The difference between a temporary inclination and a lasting change is often prayer. The difference between mediocrity and greatness is frequently prayer."*[23] The more we pray, the more God manifests His presence in our lives. The more we focus on growing and are truly passionate about our intimacy with God, the more of God's wisdom and discernment will pervade in everything we do.

Jesus on Prayer

Before the Holy Spirit came at Pentecost, *"They all joined together constantly in prayer," (Acts 1:14).* It was only when the body of believers and not a solo leader went on their knees to pray that the power and the gift of the Holy Spirit came and empowered the people to be *"witnesses in Jerusalem, and in all Judea and Samaria, and to the ends of the earth" (Acts 1:8).*

How important is prayer? Prayer was so important that it was the last thing Jesus taught his disciples before he died. If you knew you were going to die the next day, what would you teach your disciples? Jesus chose prayer as His lasting legacy, and it continues to this very day, even to you.

273

Matthew 26:36

[36] *Then Jesus went with his disciples to a place called Gethsemane, and he said to them, "Sit here while I go over there and pray."*

Jesus knew that he would die the next day, so he took his disciples to a place called Gethsemane to pray (Matt. 26:36), but when he returned to his disciples, he found them sleeping *"Couldn't you men keep watch with me for one hour?" he asked (Matt. 26:40).* Jesus told the disciples to *"watch and pray"* again in verse 41. Later, Jesus returned to find them sleeping again, *"So he left them and went away once more and prayed the third time, saying the same thing" (Matt. 26:44).* If prayer was paramount to Jesus' life and ministry, then it must be a priority for us too.

So the question is not "How is your leadership skill?" but "How is your prayer life?" Whether you're Korean, Chinese, African American, or multi-racial, being an effective leader means that prayer is THE central ingredient in your life and ministry. Prayer will always equal progress and will show you God's will. Henry and Richard Blackaby defined spiritual leadership as, *"Spiritual leadership is moving people on to God's agenda."* Furthermore, the authors urge leaders to move God's people by revelation and not by man-made visions. They state the difference as *"Vision is something people produce; revelation is something people receive. Leaders can dream up a vision, but they cannot discover God's will. God must reveal it."*[24] Then, in order to receive God's will, the leader must spend time in prayer. The leader receives the will of God and moves his followers to accomplish it. That's the responsibility of the leader.

Thoughts on Conflicts

A few years ago, my two girls were sitting next to one another enjoying the ride to a fun-filled family event. Within a few minutes an argument flared up between the two. This time I decided not to intervene to see how they would resolve the issue on their own. My older daughter drew a line in the middle of the car and told her sister not to cross the line. The other one yelled out, "Well, you too!" How silly it was to see two girls sitting next to one another not communicating nor willing to even look at each other. Yet in many ways this is how we Christians treat each other; when we face problems, we create "spiritual walls." First gen pastors prefer to keep things internal and not openly discuss ministry problems. Some may even draw a line and put a wall between them and their adversaries. In many ways this is how we resolve ministry conflicts in Asian churches. We draw spiritual lines in order to keep people from entering our comfort zone. In times of conflict leaders will disconnect and distance themselves from each other, but someone has to make the first attempt to reconnect to the spiritual family.

Many years ago, I had a conflict with a fellow pastor in the same church. We were in disagreement about how to handle a ministry matter, and our emotions got the better of us and we started to avoid one another. I soon realized that I too was drawing a line. I realized a spiritual wall was created. When another conflict arose, I went into prayer to intercede, praying for my fellow pastor to be blessed. I couldn't connect humanly, so I focused on getting connected spiritually. There's something about praying for people whom you disagree with. Christ calls all believers to love our neighbor, but practically speaking this is hard to do. However, when we ask God to bless those whom you disagree with, He changes our hearts, and we begin to feel differently toward them. Eventually, through continuous prayer, the Holy Spirit worked in my heart as well as his. My negative emotions toward the other pastor turned into a heart of compassion, so as time passed, I eventually approached him in love. The Holy Spirit re-connected our friendship, so our relationship was renewed. When conflicts occur, praying for the other person to receive the Lord's blessing opens our hearts to reconciliation. The spiritual wall and line that was drawn is now erased. We are able to fellowship with one another again, and more importantly, we are being obedient to God's great command to reconcile.

A church leader called me for help concerning a conflict at his church. As a 1.5 gen Korean American, his job was to communicate KM's agenda to the EM congregation, but a misunderstanding occurred between him and a female EM leader at his church. So, he called for some insight in dealing with this problem. I asked him a simple question, "In whatever happens and whatever the outcome will God receive the glory? After you speak to her and receive her feedback, will you be able to say, 'Lord, this was a blessed meeting.'" Whatever the conflict, issue, or problem may be in your relationship, the bottom line should be, "How can I honor God so He receives the glory?" He prayed and God answered that question. After the meeting he called to say that the meeting went very well, and that they ended with prayer. There is no better sign of reconciliation than praying together.

Church conflicts in many Asian churches are difficult to resolve. EM pastors leave, not willing to resolve the issues, but perhaps the fault doesn't lie with them alone. After all it takes two to tango. Both parties are responsible to hand the situation as righteously as possible, for the glory of God. There are no short and simple answers to many of the church conflicts that leaders face every day. But by asking the tough questions during the candidating process, we can reduce a number of conflicts related to KM and EM leadership and perhaps eliminate those that relate to boundary ambiguity and presumptive expectations. Preventing conflicts is superior to finding the best solution to conflicts, much like preventing smoking is better than coming up with a clever cure. Having pre-marital counseling dramatically improves the marriage when it begins. We pray that this book will help prevent potential issues between the FiGI churches and English ministry pastors.

In sports we chant, "We're number one! We're number one!" How awesome it would be if we, as the body of believers, could chant "We are one! We are one!" Our Lord prayed for our unity shortly before He was crucified. For what purpose? So that the unbelieving world may know that Jesus is the Messiah sent by God to reconcile the world to Himself. May we as the church demonstrate by our unity that Jesus truly lives in us.

John 17:20-24

20"I do not ask for these only, but also for those who will believe in me through their word, 21 that they may all be one, just as you, Father, are in me, and I in you, that they also may be in us, so that the world may believe that you have sent me. 22 The glory that you have given me I have given to them, that they may be one even as we are one, 23 I in them and you in me, that they may become perfectly one, so that the world may know that you sent me and loved them even as you loved me. 24Father, I desire that they also, whom you have given me, may be with me where I am, to see my glory that you have given me because you loved me before the foundation of the world.

Appendix A

Sample EM Pastor Job Description

EM Pastor Position Summary: The EM pastor is responsible for providing the senior leadership and oversight of the English Ministry, youth, and children's ministry. The primary role of the EM pastor is to assist the elders in overseeing the life and direction of the English Ministry. The EM pastor will have a solid understanding of the head church's vision, mission, and strategy and the ability to align ordained leaders and lay staff and key leadership teams with its mission and purpose. The EM pastor will work in harmony with the senior pastor and will ensure that the systems, practices, and policies of the church responsibly and effectively support its ministry activities. The EM pastor will work alongside other pastors and lay ministers to carry out the mission as a team.

EXPECTATIONS: The EM pastor is expected to grasp and apply the head church's vision and implement its core missions and values in the English Ministry. We will expect the EM pastor's spouse to be part of the English Ministry team in a supportive role. We expect spiritual and professional growth in strategic areas, while being a part of the overall church team. The head church will provide a certain amount of spiritual growth opportunities through conferences, seminars, and/or leadership training programs. We expect the EM pastor to be part of the early morning prayers every Tuesday and Thursday with exceptions on special agenda days and conferences. The EM pastor must attend weekly staff meetings and report to the elders of the church once per month.

SUPERVISOR: The EM pastor is primarily accountable to the senior pastor and will give him direct reports, strategies, and plans for review and confirmation. To eliminate any miscommunication in a bi-cultural ministry, including language differences, the head church will assign a bilingual 1.5 gen lay leader to the English Ministry as the "bridge," if the EM pastor does not speak the native language. The 1.5 gen lay leader will work alongside the EM pastor and help establish a line of communication with the 1st gen senior pastor.

PRIMARY RESPONSIBILITES:

PREACHING AND TEACHING: The EM pastor will be the primary preacher for Sunday worship services. The pastor will also provide leadership in planning and executing the different programs for Bible study, small groups, membership classes, and leadership training in coordination with other lay leaders.

STRATEGIC PLANNING: The EM pastor will define and implement strategic goals for the English Ministry. The EM pastor will coordinate weekly lay leadership training and other activities to develop leaders and clarify the direction of the ministry. The EM pastor will lead corporate prayer times and fasts when needed for spiritual direction.

SUPERVISION and DEVELOPMENT: The EM pastor will oversee the youth and elementary ministry and provide personnel and/or lay leaders support, wise counsel, and resources toward the church mission and goals. The pastor will further provide leadership to the youth and children's ministers in the design and implementation of programs. The pastor will also oversee EM lay leaders' training, recruitment, and development. The EM pastor will identify potential small, life, or cell group leaders and implement leadership development through informal and formal methods. The pastor will maintain efficient and effective lines of communication with senior leadership and EM lay leaders.

OTHER FUNCTIONS: The EM pastor will conduct weddings, funerals, and general counseling as needed by the English Ministry. The EM pastor will also administer communion, perform baptisms, baby dedications, hospital visitations, home visits, and address member conflicts. The EM pastor will work along with local Christian counseling services to direct people of special needs only if the pastor has not been trained in Christian counseling service. He will meet as needed with the team under the senior pastor's direction to provide support, encouragement, training, accountability, and direction for all ministries of the church. He will give support and provide direction, as needed, for the effective service of the front office.

EVALUATION AND COMPENSATION: The EM pastor will file quarterly reports with the senior pastor and when requested file reports to the elders on ministry accomplishments and activities. With the senior pastor's participation the personnel team will conduct annually a performance evaluation and review the compensation package.

[Optional]

I have read and received a copy of my job description. I understand this overrides anything I have been given or told in the past. I further understand that I am expected to follow my job as outlined above, and that if I have any questions concerning what is expected of me, I will speak with my immediate supervisor as identified above.

Print Name: _____

Sign: _____

Date: _____

Appendix B

Sample Questions to Pastoral Candidate

[Sample: Associate Pastor / Teaching Pastor]

Questionnaire:

1. What about this position interests you?

2. Who are a few of your favorite communicators and why?

3. Describe your greatest leadership strengths:

   Greatest leadership liabilities:

4. How would you define a healthy church?

5. What are two or three greatest challenges that you have faced in the last ten years?

6. Describe a time in your life that uniquely prompted your spiritual growth and share some of the things you learned.

7. Outside of the Bible, briefly discuss three books that have had a significant impact on you.

8. What do you enjoy doing in your leisure time?

9. Are there other media, beyond the audio files of sermons you will include with this application, that will help us get to know you better? (ex: blogs / website/ podcast / etc.)

[Sample: Executive / Administrative Pastor]

Questionnaire:

___Yes ___ No I have read about (Church Name) from (website).

(If the following items are not already in your resume, please include them with this form)

Why do you want to work for (Church Name)?

FAITH

1. Tell us how you came to faith in Christ.

2. Briefly describe how one would see your love for Christ.

3. Comment on your personal devotional life.

4. What do you think are your spiritual gifts?

5. Can you affirm our VALUES as seen on our website? If not completely, what areas are problematic for you?

6. What is your denomination/heritage?

7. What part of shepherding people do you enjoy most?

8. What did you enjoy most about your last position?

    What did you enjoy least?

9. The Executive Pastor's role can be fashioned in many ways. Divide the focus you as Executive Pastor would expect to have on these various roles (ex: 25% this, 50% that, 25% other) and why.

    Chief of Staff _____ %
    Chief Operating Officer _____ %
    Chief Financial Officer _____%
    Other (describe) _____ %

10. What experience do you bring that would let you excel in any of these areas?

11. In your opinion what role should the Executive Pastor have in these ministry areas?

    Funerals:
    Weddings:
    Preaching:
    Teaching:

12. How do you keep yourself current?

13. If you could create your "ideal" Executive Pastor position, what would it look like?

14. The Executive Pastor will have authority over our pastors. Many of these pastors are ordained. Do you have any theological training? Are you ordained? If not, how will you work with this dynamic?

15. Describe the relationship you as Executive Pastor had with your previous senior pastor(s), and how would you improve on this with this new position?

LEADERSHIP

16. Describe the growth of your staff under your leadership.

17. Describe your style of leadership. Have you taken any assessments? (DISC, etc.)

18. What exemplifies good leadership?

19. Tell us of a conflict between two staff members and the part you played to see it resolved.

20. How do you prioritize & keep track of your objectives?

21. How do you hold staff accountable without creating conflict?

Bold and <u>Underline</u> the number in the continuum that best shows your position or preferences:

Executive Pastor Role:
   Very public 1 2 3 4 5 6 7 8 9 10 Behind the scenes

Experience in multi-site churches:
   Never 1 2 3 4 5 6 7 8 9 10 Been there

Theology:
   Liberal 0 1 2 3 4 5 6 7 8 9 10 Conservative

Women in leadership:
   No Problem 0 1 2 3 4 5 6 7 8 9 10 Can't see it

Experience in managing staff:
   No Experience 0 1 2 3 4 5 6 7 8 9 10 Lots

Can challenge people to improve their ministry:
   Not my thing 1 2 3 4 5 6 7 8 9 10 Effectively

Have hired & fired church or business employees:
   Never 0 1 2 3 4 5 6 7 8 9 10 Very capable

Have reviewed staff [Have done in the past]:
   Never 0 1 2 3 4 5 6 7 8 9 10 Lots

Oversee budget compliance [Have done in the past]
   Never 0 1 2 3 4 5 6 7 8 9 10 Lots

Chief of Staff role [Have done in the past]:
   Delegate to admin person 0 1 2 3 4 5 6 7 8 9 10 I do that

Chief Operating Officer [Have done in the past]
   Delegate to subordinate 0 1 2 3 4 5 6 7 8 9 10 I do that

Chief Financial Officer [Have done in the past]:
Delegate to subordinate 0 1 2 3 4 5 6 7 8 9 10 I do that

Strategy [Question on "I dream it up?]:
Rather implement a defined strategy 1 2 3 4 5 6 7 8 9 10 I dream it up

Volunteers:
Paid staff preferred 1 2 3 4 5 6 7 8 9 10 Love getting them involved

Manage ministries:
Delegate 0 1 2 3 4 5 6 7 8 9 10 Very hands on

Ministry volunteers & Christians:
Not Req. 0 1 2 3 4 5 6 7 8 9 10 Must be Christians

Ministry volunteers & membership:
Not Req. 0 1 2 3 4 5 6 7 8 9 10 Must be Members

Leadership should be paid staff:
Never 0 1 2 3 4 5 6 7 8 9 10 Always

Worship music style preferred:
Traditional 1 2 3 4 5 6 7 8 9 10 Contemporary

Appendix C

Performance Evaluation Form

[Sample Performance Evaluation Form]

The person being evaluated must give to the supervisor, executive pastor, or senior pastor at least three different names that the "employee" is working with in their ministry context. For example, the EM pastor will be evaluated by: a worship leader, deacon or elder, associate pastor, ministry leader, and other ministers or pastors, and should be given these forms for them to do an evaluation of the EM pastor. The evaluation is not done by a supervisor or any person overseeing the "employee." Please make sure that the names of the people that are doing the evaluation are not indicated. The evaluation forms are given to different ministry leaders, then sent back via email, then copied and pasted to compile the information to be reviewed by the supervisor or primary employer of the church. All information is kept confidential because the objective is to help and develop the leaders from a Christian perspective in a positive tone. A time frame of one week should be given for the forms to be filled and the second week to be compiled by a person that will keep the information confidential. Once the information is compiled, it then needs to be given to the supervisor and "employee" to be reviewed.

Front Cover

Pastoral Employee
Performance Evaluation

Pastor's Name:
Title:
Hired Date:
Last Evaluation Date:

Period Covered in this Evaluation:
Reviewed by:
Date of Review:

Next Page

Rating Scale:

5   Excellent – Performance exceeds congregation's expectations. Achievement is the result of unique performance and is clearly recognized as outstanding.

4   Good – Performance consistently exceeds requirements. Overall performance exceeds objectives.

3   Average – Performance consistently meets, but does not exceed, expectations for this position.

2   Needs Improvement – Performance does not meet expected levels. Improvement is necessary.

1   Not Acceptable – Performance does not meet expected levels. Overall performance must improve immediately.

[Please keep written answers brief but clear enough to discuss with employee during evaluation with supervisor.]

PASTORAL & SPIRITUAL SKILLS: Average Score _____

1. **Is attentive and responsive** in meeting the spiritual needs of the congregation.
Rating: _____
Comments: [Sample]
   - *Spirit led in providing care, spiritual direction, and prayer support. Strong evangelist. Great listener. Good heart.*

- *Very knowledgeable about Scripture.*

2. **Establishes sound working** relationships and cooperative arrangements with the congregation, ministry leaders, other pastors, and the local community.
Rating: _____
Comments: [Sample]
   - *Other leaders and staff members like him but I am not sure they have the highest respect for him.*
   - *He extends pastoral care to persons seeking spiritual guidance, e.g., recently a gentleman just released ...*

3. **Provides leadership in** developing programs and plans with the appropriate ministry leaders.
Rating: _____
Comments:

4. **Serves as an effective ambassador** and spokesperson for (Church name). Demonstrates a commitment to honor and uphold the values and doctrine of the church.
Rating: _____
Comments:

5. **Works well with** the elders, pastors, and leadership of (Church name).
Rating: _____
Comments:

6. **Manages own** time effectively to maintain a healthy balance in personal/family/congregational life.
Rating: _____
Comments:

7. **Seeks to model Christian life** and exhibits the fruit of the Spirit (love, joy, peace, patience, kindness, goodness, faithfulness, gentleness and self-control). Gal 5:22-23

Rating: _____
Comments:

LEADERSHIP PRACTICES: Average Score _____

1. **Communication** – Open and honest in his communication; have effective processes in place for communicating news, strategies, and goals to employees; ensures that employees know what is expected of them. Maintains an optimistic communication style.
   Rating: _____
   Comments: [Sample]
   - *May seek input but doesn't necessarily use it.*
   - *Communicates and expresses ideas well.*
   - *Needs to use fewer words when responding in meetings.*
   - *Needs to think through thoughts and work on communicating clearly.*
   - *Needs to work on being honest and open earlier in conversations so follow-up conversations can occur on any issues.*
   - *Shares ideas for improvement and solicits comments from team members.*

2. **Inclusiveness** – Seeks and uses employee input; works in partnership with employees; and treats them with respect.
   Rating: _____
   Comments: [Sample]
   - *Uses critical thinking for ways to increase giving to the various ministries.*
   - *Seeks advice regarding certain ideas.*
   - *Tends to go off and do his own thing without consulting with his supervisor or other employees*

3. **Flexibility** – Values and respects diverse opinions, experiences, background, cultures, and work styles; identifies, shares, and is

receptive to new ideas; adapts to new situations; helps others overcome resistance to change; resolves conflicts gracefully.
Rating: _____
Comments:

- *Communicates well in resolving conflict.*
- *Sometimes gives the impression of being flexible but then moves forward with his own plans.*
- *Very good at finding solutions to issues*

4. **Supervisory Skills** – Demonstrates organizational values; eliminates unnecessary barriers to getting work done; offers constructive feedback; provides employees with performance appraisals; sets SMART (Specific, Measurable, Actionable, Realistic, Timed) goals; measures outcomes; and inspires confidence.
Rating: _____
Comments:

- *Does most of this well. He has gotten very good at encouraging employees in their work and in their craft.*
- *Usually gives great feedback when something is done well and also gives criticisms gracefully when something needs to change.*
- *Sometimes the lack of communication creates unnecessary barriers in getting work done.*

5. **Executive Skills** – Provides a clear vision for his/her area of responsibility and outlines strategies and tactics for accomplishing that vision. Adjusts regularly based on changes and feedback. Delegates work appropriately and maintains high visibility within the organization.
Rating: _____
Comments:

- *Weak at delegating the Missions Café work and training new leader and staff in timely manner.*
- *Good at communicating vision and implementing strategies.*

EMPLOYEE ENGAGEMENT: Average Score _____

1. **Job Design** – Work is effectively organized; makes good use of employees' talents and skills, and is interesting and meaningful. Employees are given appropriate responsibility to determine how best to do their work and jobs are designed to help make jobs fit employees' needs.
   Rating: _____
   Comments:

2. **Commitment to Employees** – Employees are made to feel secure in their jobs, recognized for their accomplishments and provided with opportunity for growth.
   Rating: _____
   Comments:

3. **Time** – The workload allows employees to do their jobs well, make thoughtful decisions, and achieve appropriate balance between work and home.
   Rating: _____
   Comments:

KNOWLEDGE ACCESSIBILITY: Average Score _____

1. **Availability** – Employees are provided with necessary information they need to do their jobs. Training is also discussed and available as needed.
   Rating: _____
   Comments:

2. **Collaboration & Teamwork** – Teamwork is encouraged and facilitated and time is set aside for employees to share with and learn from one another.
   Rating: _____
   Comments:

3. **Information Sharing** – Best practices and tips shared, improved, and circulated across departments.
   Rating: _____
   Comments:

WORKFORCE OPTIMIZATION: Average Score _____

1. **Processes** – Processes for getting work done are well defined and continually improved; and employees are well trained in how to use them.
   Rating: _____
   Comments:

2. **Conditions** – Employees have access to the resources they need and working conditions contribute to good performance.
   Rating: _____
   Comments:

LEARNING CAPACITY: Average Score _____

1. **Innovation** – New ideas are welcomed, employees are encouraged to find new and better ways to work, and employees' input is sought in solving problems.
   Ratings: _____
   Comments:

2. **Training/Growth** – Employee training and growth plans are practical, supports organizational goals, and is provided for work – related topics.
   Ratings: _____
   Comments:

3. **Development** – Employees are given formal development plans and those plans are used to achieve their career goals.
   Ratings: _____
   Comments:

SUMMARY OF STRENGTHS
[Sample]
- Has great spirit and energy, making him very dependable.
- Loves the Lord and communicates this well in personal life.
- Positive attitude.
- (Name) demonstrates the ability to easily gain the confidence of others, especially total strangers.

NEEDS IMPROVEMENT IN:
[Sample]
- Organizational skills
- Leadership development
- Communication – open, honest, clear
- Stop passive-aggressive approaches

Organizational Steps to Improve [Discussions with supervisor]

[Sample]

- (Name) will start working on one hour prayer for 30 days straight
- (Name) will start journaling concerning spiritual growth
- (Name) will take classes on relational conflicts and how to manage stress and anger issues.
- (Name) will start spending more time with family starting on (date).

Pastor's Signature_____

Date. _____

Supervisor's Signature _____

Date: _____

Appendix D

Vision, Mission, Core Values, & Strategy
Samples

Vision:

Sample 1: "(Church Name) is to be a multicultural army of fully-devoted followers of Christ moving forward in unity and love to reach our community, our culture, and our world for Jesus Christ."

Sample 2; "We see (Church Name) as a dynamic, spirit-filled, multi-cultural church, numbering in the thousands, impacting our city, our nation, and our world through leadership development and church planting."

Mission:

Sample 1: "We are to build into one another as we build bridges to our community."

Sample 2: "(Church Name) is called to proclaim the gospel of Christ and the beliefs of the evangelical Christian faith, to maintain the worship of God, and to inspire in all persons a love for Christ, a passion for righteousness, and a consciousness of their duties to God and their fellow human beings. We pledge our lives to Christ and covenant with each other to demonstrate His Spirit through worship, witnessing, and ministry to the needs of the people of this church and the community.

Core Values:

Sample 1: B.R.I.D.G.E.S.

Building into One Another
Reconciliation—Spiritually, Racially, and Relationally
Instruction
Dynamic Worship
Growth—Personally & Spiritually
Evangelism
Service/Stewardship

Sample 2: The following represents the core values that (Church Name) is passionate about and aspire to which reflects the very essence of who we are as a church:

1. Biblical Teaching: We lead people out of a deep conviction and commitment to God's Word, so that together we grow in our love and application of it.

2. Biblical Worship: We glorify God and experience His presence through corporate and personal worship that is God centered, life changing and based on biblical principles, resulting in expressions of gratitude, honor, and service.

3. Prayer: We elevate communication with God as an essential means for personal transformation and effective ministry, which pleases and honors Him.

4. Evangelism: We actively build relationships with non- believers to communicate the gospel of Jesus Christ through word and deed, both locally and globally.

5. Equipping & Multiplying Disciples: We equip followers of Christ to cultivate their spiritual lives in order to nurture Christ likeness and reproduce ministry in others.

6. Biblical Community: We intentionally facilitate nurturing community environments where we encourage, challenge, and hold each other accountable in the process of spiritual growth and Christ-like relationships.

7. Servant Leadership: We reproduce servant leaders who are committed to ministry teams and dependence on God's word, the Holy Spirit, and one another. This begins with the elders, who have the final responsibility for guiding and shepherding our congregation, and continues to all ministries.

Strategy:

Sample 1: connect-build-equip-lead

This strategy of progression in developing fully-devoted followers of Christ is demonstrated in programs with the primary purposes of outreach, growth/in reach, ministry training, and leadership development.

> **Connect:** Helping people connect to Christ, our church, and each other AND help the church connect to the community.
>
> **Build:** Helping others grow in their walk as fully devoted followers of Christ through the Word, worship, prayer, fellowship, & sharing.
>
> **Equip:** Helping others grow in their walk as fully devoted followers of Christ AND helping them see ministry to others as a natural outgrowth of that walk.
>
> **Lead:** Helping others grow in their walk AND helping them lead "committed" people (leaders who make other fully devoted Christ followers).

Sample 2:

The following strategic goals provide the overarching direction for how we as a congregation will proceed in order to achieve our vision. These goals and objectives were derived from interviews with leaders in our congregation as well as from information gathered from the congregation at large and through questionnaires and interviews with leaders of the church's various working committees.

1. Nurture spiritual growth: We will provide and increase opportunities to enrich the spiritual growth of our members and friends of all ages.

2. Cultivate membership participation: We will promote the growth of our congregation, cultivating new members, volunteers, and church leaders while remaining mindful of the needs of current members and friends.

3. Engage within and reach out beyond our changing community: We will become a vital voice in the larger communities beyond our church by increasing our outreach, service, and social action efforts.

4. Provide good stewardship of our property: We will restore and maintain our buildings and grounds to a condition that will best facilitate the ministry and fellowship goals of the congregation.

5. Act and communicate effectively in all congregation activities: We will organize our governing and communication practices to serve our committees and the congregation at large most efficiently.

6. Provide sufficient resources of money and staff: We will creatively address the short and long-term financial and staffing needs of the church and provide the resources to achieve those needs while fostering a mindset of abundance.

7. Measure our progress: We will commit resources to establish and regularly use feedback mechanisms and tracking tools to measure our overall progress toward achieving our objectives, goals, and vision.

Appendix E

Research on Young Adults Ministry

Sample Research Application

When I first came on board with a large American church, I did a detailed analysis on the pillars of the church. Pillars of the church are typically long-term ministries that support the primary function and operations of the church. Examples of pillars are such as children, youth, men's, and women's ministries. As the church grows, other pillars need to be planted for longevity and further growth. One of the pillars I noticed that was missing was the young adults ministry. There was a singles ministry, but it primarily consisted of people ages 45 to 55.

1. My first response was to study the congregation and determine the makeup for a potential ministry.

2. I spoke with over 10 young adults in their 20s and 30s to see what their thoughts were about a potential ministry just for them.

3. I then spoke with the leadership team who has been at the church for a length of time to see if in the past, if there ever was a young adults ministry and who was in charge. I discovered from the interviews that a young adults ministry did exist and the person that who was in charge of it was still present.

4. The interview with this person went very well. I took detailed notes on why they started it in the first place, how did they try to promote it, what worked, what didn't work, and why they stopped this ministry.

5. I then decided to contact five churches that were similar in culture and context to find out if they had a young adults ministry.

From the five an evaluation was done to determine the size of the young adult groups and the congregation. I began first with a phone interview of a small young adult group. Then did a personal interview on a mid-size group that had a congregation size of over 2,000 people. The third group consisted of a congregation size of over 5,000 people. The reason for this was to understand what the young adults ministry would look like in three to five years.

7. Following is the actual report for the young adults ministry:

[Research]

Church Research into Young Adults Ministry (YAM)
Initial Research
By Joseph Choi

Overarching Goal: Come up with the best probability on what the young adults ministry would look like in the beginning, growing, and maturing stage for the young adults ministry.

Three churches were looked at that would most resemble the dynamics, environment, and structure somewhat similar to (Church Name). The following three churches were chosen: (Church 1), (Church 2), and (Church 3).

1st Interview with Church 1

Name: _____ Phone No: _____
Email: _____

YAM: (Group Name)
Age Range: 18 – 25
Size: 15-18
Existed: 2 Years

YAM: They desire authentic relationships

- Honesty with answers
- Community and acceptance
- Involvement in service
- Transparency
- The leaders to invest time and energy
- Solid line of communication with senior leaders to stay in touch with what they're doing in the ministry. (Constant reporting of progress is crucial to the long term success of Young Adults Ministry (YAM)).

For the Leaders: Have an open door policy, but make sure everyone knows the boundaries. The young adults would like to see a healthy family; it's part of their goals in life.

Beginnings: There were some leaders who ran the program before, but the leaders/ministers were the same age as the YAM. In other words they were lacking in maturity and life experience to make an impact on YAM. The couple came in when things were falling apart.

The first 6 months were focused on healing from the problems of previous church leadership and other issues. Afterwards:

1. Fellowship and worship was emphasized strongly.
2. Open Mics was an important theme.
   a. Reaching the people's heart
   b. Stirring the heart and playing devil's advocate challenged their minds.
   c. Creating a wider faith
   d. Really biting into what they believed and why they believed it.
   e. Played with politics and how the church played into their lives.
   f. People signed up to read poems, sing songs, show their talents, play music among others. (non-believers came to know the church and the people)
3. Missionaries came and did some speaking.
4. Reconciliation Ministry was a key factor.

5. In the second year they ran some leadership training programs as well as gifts inventories.
6. They focused on "Sharing the heart"
7. Also did healing ministry.

(Church 2)

Coordinator's	(Names)
Age Range:	18-30 (Some are in there older 30's)
Size:	Around 300 or more
Group Name:	Axis
Small Groups:	Meets every Thursday at 7pm
Worship Service:	Worship Service every 3rd Thursday at 7pm
Departments:	Singles (Men and Women)
	College
	Couples
	Spanish
	Young Women

Interview with Pastor:

J: Did you ever have a young adults ministry (YAM) before?

Pastor: Young adults ministry (YAM) was in operations before. Once, the leader left, the ministry stopped. I was in YAM at first before I took over.

J: What did the previous YAM look like?

Steve: They just had weekly service at 7 pm with worship and message. Afterwards, we had fellowship.

J: What were other things that you guys had done?

Pastor: Occasionally we had activities such as bowling and meeting together for fellowship at restaurants and so forth.

J: Were there any small groups during this time?

Pastor: No. I wish we had small groups for YAM. It would've made a very big difference. We now have small groups for YAM because of the effectiveness in growth.

J: What were the numbers of the previous YAM?

Pastor: We started around 70 to 100 people but then towards the end of about 5 to 6 months, the number dwindled down to about 20 to 30 people.

J: How were people getting connected with the previous YAM?

Pastor: Really no connections. After worship service on Sundays, friends just hung around and chatted. There was no real point of connection.

J: What was the first change?

Pastor: Developing a theme. The focus was to grow in relationship with God and develop relationships with one another as accountability partners. What I noticed was that getting carried away with social themes was not good for YAM. Instead of just a gathering we wanted something more authentic in building one another up. The first step I took was to find leaders and build them up to be ready to teach small groups. Once the small group grew to about 50 members then I started a worship service just for YAM. It's very important for the leaders to have worship service just for YAM members in working towards evangelism. I first started off with 8-10 leaders. I had started a small group with them first going over many different facets of leadership and building relationships. We started to meet every Thursday night at 7 at the church. We shared God's words and had fellowship. Slowly people began to add to our group. A year later we now have 4 small groups.

1. Couples
2. Singles (Men and women)
3. College

4. Spanish

The leaders will mostly meet on Thursday nights, but some small groups with the leaders will meet on a different night or just meet before or after church. Currently we have 12 people training to become the next small group leaders. We have a manual and a study guide for the leaders but not the small group members. This is a six week course training for the leaders.

I get most of my material from Serendipity (Publishing Warehouse) that sell leadership books and bunch of others.

(Church 3)

Name: (Group Name)
Worship: Every Sunday at 5:30 service
                Online Campus – Connect Direct
Age Range: 20s and 30s
Size: Few thousand (Over 2,000 young adults)

Departments: -   Group Name: College Students
                -   Group Name: Singles 20s and 30s:
                -   (Meetings on Sunday Morning)
                -   The Group Name: Couples 20s and 30s,
                    (Meeting on Sunday Mornings)
                -   The Group Name: Couples 20s and 30s,
                    (Meeting on Sunday Evenings)
                -   Young adults with special needs (Meeting on
                    Sunday evenings)
                -   Preparing for marriage class (for engaged
                    couples)
                -   Parenting resources
                -   Future leaders program

Interview with leaders

                -   members as a singles
                -   moved to apprentice

- moved to small group leadership
- both became coaches
- (Name) became a senior coach
- Got married and moved to young couples small group

The Interview about YAM small group leaders

Question: How did you find out about the YAM in your church?

Response: They made an announcement at the beginning of service saying things like, "If you're new to us, please join us for a welcome meeting, and we have a free gift for you. Or they might also say, "These are ministries we have and it's a great way for you to get connected," and they would explain it briefly. But what I noticed is that a lot of people go because of the free gift, I mean who doesn't like free gifts. The primary goal of the Welcome Center is to have you fill out a form which asks for name, age, address, maturity level as a Christian, and what you're interested in. Within one week you'll get a call from (Church name) and they will ask if you are interested in joining a small group. The goal of (Church name) is to plug you in as quickly as possible to a small group to make you feel that you are important, and the church has a community for you.

Question: What if you don't like the small group?

Response: In the beginning when they call you, they will let you know right off the bat that if you don't feel comfortable, they will find you another small group, but they encourage you to try it for at least 2 to 3 times. Rarely, will they have any problems, but still the goal is to try to find the right community for the individual.

Question: What are the small groups like, environmentally and culturally?

Response: Small groups are divided into many different categories of small groups. The culture was to love and accept all. The environment for the women would always have some type of desert or something. Around 2 to 3 people would always bring something to eat and snack on. Since all the small groups gather at someone's home, this really helped to have an open atmosphere for fellowship and sharing instead just studying. The objective was to start with prayer, sharing and testimonies, Bible study, praying for one another, and close with prayer. However, things would change depending on the situation of the small group issues such as at one time we had a friend in our group who moved in with a guy before marriage and they broke up and her heart was turning towards, the guy again, but we stayed accountable with her and gave her courage to overcome in the meeting as well as to assign other members to constantly call her.

Key words that I have heard from all the church leaders:

- Community
- Acceptance
- Small group
- Seeking openness
- Seeking truths
- Connecting with people

From Leaders

- Hit the mind
- Challenge
- Accountability
- Leave no one isolated
- Seek out resources for out of darkness
- Open and transparent
- Encourage service

7 Characteristics of a Successful Young Adults Ministry

According to Rodger Nishioka, Associate Professor of Christian Education at Columbia Presbyterian Seminary in Atlanta, Georgia, congregations doing significant young adults ministry exhibit 7 characteristics:

1. The church invites responsibility, gives it, and shares power with young adults.

2. The congregation focuses on a faith that delivers relevance over and over, Sunday after Sunday. It makes central the questions, "What does this text have to do with me?"

3. The congregation creates meaningful opportunities for belonging through specific groups for just young adults, labeled for the age group.

4. The church is linked to the larger community in tangible ways.

5. The congregation is sensitive to outsiders and avoids coded language and interprets its codes when used, not assuming newcomers know the meaning of liturgical terms, for example.

6. The congregation provides imagery for practicing faith and ways to live, images of a positive self, of what "cannot be allowed" (what harms people and creation) and images that evoke wonder, mystery and awe.

7. The church worships with passion and excitement and delivers compelling, even costly messages of Jesus Christ.

With the completion of this research and giving the data to the leaders, the new ministry began with a great strategic outlook. The research brought about clear boundaries of responsibilities, clarity of expectations, roles for the starting core team, and a strong mission.

I'm in my _____ year of ministry. Is it still too late to do this?

Absolutely Not! First through prayer and by the leading of the Holy Spirit a pastor can discern if the desired changes are right for him right now. Many pastors can attend seminars and conferences and get excited about a unique program without realizing if it fits into his own identity. Pushing a program normally will mean that the pastor will work alone, but a prayer-led ministry is always supported by God.

It is important though, that the changes are not done solely by the pastor but in accordance with the core team. All team members, including elders and superiors that play a key role in the EM, should pray about the conviction of the EM pastor's new ministry focus. Moving in a new direction and finding success requires team effort.

Author

Joseph Y. Choi is the co-founder of JnJ Publishing House, whose vision is to provide ministry resources that are "Real, Practical, and Supernatural" for the next gen. He attended Golden Gate, Denver, and Liberty Baptist Theological seminaries. He is co-author of *New Beginning I've accepted Christ – now what?* Further book projects on *Real People Real Suffering Real Victory*, *Men of Integrity* and *Supernatural* will be released in the near future. As speaker, author, and pastor, Joseph Choi's passion in life is to reach lost souls for Jesus Christ.

Co-author

W. Jae Lee is the co-founder of JnJ Publishing House and is the chief editor. He is co-author of *New Beginning I've accepted Christ – now what?* Further book projects on *Real People Real Suffering Real Victory*, *Men of Integrity* and *Supernatural* will be released in the near future. After working as an Electrical Engineer for two years, he entered Dallas Theological Seminary and graduated with a Masters of Theology in Family Ministry. His passion for the family and the church is evident not only in his own family with wife and 6 children, but his emphasis and teaching on the subject in every area of ministry.

Acknowledgments

Joseph: First and foremost, I want to acknowledge the mercy and grace of God who has allowed me a deeper, richer, and more intimate relationship with the Lord Jesus Christ. With the titanic task of completing this book while working as a full time pastor and being a father and husband, I was strengthened when the Lord intervened to bring me many prayer warriors in order to help me complete this book. Thanks goes to my wife Jackie and my children Grace, Ashleigh, and Colin along with many others who have faithfully and frequently prayed for me so that I could complete this project. Without their prayers, I could not have finished this monumental undertaking.

Jae: Praise the Lord who has given me the opportunity to express my teaching gift through writing. Although I have always had the ambition to write, it wasn't until I met Joseph that the Lord combined the gift with the medium. I would like to thank my wife Sue Jean and children: Simeon, Hope, Jonah, Isaac, Elijah, and Moses who encouraged me to write my stories into a book.

Our sincere gratitude goes to our cover designer Ann Pak who is a freelance photographer and public school teacher in Maryland. She is passionate about God's love and beauty in all things and shares her passion through a creative lens. She donated her time and talent to produce the beautiful cover you are holding in your hands. Please visit http://annyphotography.com to see her other masterpieces.

Finally, we would like to thank you for buying and reading this book. We pray that this book will serve its purpose in reducing church conflicts. May the LORD bless you in your endeavor to grow to be more like Christ.

To order this book and others, go to **JnJpublishing.com**
(discounts available directly from JnJpublishing.com website)
or Amazon.com
For questions and comments, go to JnJpublishing.com or
email us directly at **JnJpublishinghouse@gmail.com**

Thank you for ordering

New Beginning
I've Accepted Christ – now what?

Hiring an
English Ministry Pastor
& Beyond
In an Asian American Church context

Coming Soon:

Real People Real Suffering Real Victory

Men of Integrity (M.O.I)
Wise Counsel to a Fatherless Generation

Supernatural
Do you believe?

[1] K. Connie Kang, "Asian American churches face leadership gap," Los Angeles Times, March 03, 2007.

[2] Ibid.

[3] George Barna, *THE POWER OF TEAM LEADERSHIP: Finding Strength in Shared Responsibility* (Colorado Springs, Colorado: WaterBrook Press, 2001), 17.

[4] Compassion International, www.compassion.com (July 19, 2010).

[5] David A. Anderson, *Multicultural Ministry* (Grand Rapids, MI: Zondervan, 2004), 30.

[6] Ibid., 9.

[7] Jin Han and Cameron Lee "Ministry Demand and Stress Among Korean American Pastors: A Brief Report." Pastoral Psychology, Vol. 52, No. 6, July 2004: 173-178.

[8] Barna, *THE POWER OF TEAM LEADERSHIP*, 2-3.

[9] Ibid., 4-5.

[10] Wayne Cordeiro, "Building Church Leaders. 'Ask the Experts Disussion: Wayne Cordeiro'" July 13, 2010, http://www.buildingchurchleaders.com/help/asktheexperts/waynecordeir o/q5.html, (July 25, 2010).

[11] Peter Hyun, *Man Sei! The Making of a Korean American* (Honolulu, Hawaii: University of Hawaii Press, 1986), 27.

[12] Willard F. Harley, *His Needs Her Needs: Building an Affair-Proof Marriage* (Grand Rapids, MI: Baker Book House Company, 2001), 15.

[13] John R. Cionca, *Before You Move: A guide to Making Transitions in Ministry* (Grand Rapids, MI: Kregel Publication, 2004), 22.

[14] Official USDA Food Plans: Cost of Food at Home at Four Levels, U.S. Average, August 2007, http://www.cnpp.usda.gov/Publications/FoodPlans/2007/CostofFoodAug0 7.pdf (July 24, 2010).

[15] Richard R. Hammar, *The 2009 Compensation Handbook for Church Staff*, Surveyed between January and March by Your Church Media Group at Christianity Today International, 2009.

[16] U.S. Census Bureau, "The 2010 Statistical Abstract: The National Data Book," Educational Attainment. http://www.census.gov/compendia/statab/cats/education.html (July 26, 2010).

[17] James Rickard, "The Pastor and His Salary Package" Issue January / February 2009 by Baptist bulletin, 2009 Regular Baptist Press.

[18] Vernon Brewer, *Children of Hope* (Forest, Virginia: World Help, Inc., 2007), 11.

[19] Allen Kim, "Schooling Fathers," KoreAm, June 1, 2009, http://iamkoream.com/schooling-fathers/ August 4, 2010.

[20] Victor Lee, "A VISION FOR THE NEW MILLENIUM: Growing English Ministries," Revised Version April 2000.

[21] John Tung, "Leadership in the Asian Church," Chinese Bible Church of Maryland (CBCM), interview by author, July 30, 2010.

[22] Choi, Joseph Y, and W. Jae Lee. *New Beginning I've Accepted Christ – Now What?: A Discipleship Guide For New Believers.* Maryland: JnJ Publishing House, 2011.

[23] Earley, Dave. Prayer: *The Timeless Secret of High-Impact Leaders.* Chattanooga, TN: Living Ink Books, 2008.

[24] Blackaby, Henry, and Richard Blackaby. *Spiritual Leadership: Moving People on to God's Agenda.* Nashville, TN: Broadman & Holman Publishers, 2001.

Made in the USA
Lexington, KY
21 February 2012